Also by Kary Oberbrunner

Poetry is the Portal

Blockchain Life

Your Book is Not a Business Card

Show Up Filled Up

Unhackable

Elixir Project

Day Job to Dream Job

The Deeper Path

Your Secret Name

The Fine Line

Called

The Journey Towards Relevance

THE E-MIND

How to Think Like an Entrepreneur
and Gain an Exponential Advantage

THE E-MIND

How to Think Like an Entrepreneur and Gain an Exponential Advantage

Dr. Kary Oberbrunner

Lynne Modranski

Printed in the United States of America

Published by Ethos Collective™
PO Box 43, Powell, OH 43065
www.ethoscollective.vip

LCCN: 2023914018
Paperback ISBN: 978-1-63680-190-2
Hardcover ISBN: 978-1-63680-191-9
e-book ISBN: 978-1-63680-192-6

Available in paperback, hardcover, e-book, and audiobook.

Dedication

To Cedarville University.
Thanks for allowing me to fulfill my mission:
Igniting Souls by Setting Free World Changing Ideas.
It's an honor to serve your incredible entrepreneurs.

And especially to Dr. Jeffrey Haymond.
Thanks for your flexibility in making
this a successful collaboration.

Contents

Foreword

I don't need to convince you.

The world is increasingly moving toward a brand new abundant future. The daily upgrades are palpable—computation, knowledge, and access to global experts—capabilities that were once only available to heads of nations and global CEOs are now available to anyone online.

We'll experience more change this coming decade than we have in the entire past century. Converging exponential technologies like AI, robotics, and biotech are disrupting and reinventing every industry and business model.

So how do we respond?

Kary Oberbrunner and I share a common belief: we need to change the way we think about change.

WE NEED TO CHANGE THE WAY WE THINK ABOUT CHANGE.

The people who try to ignore change will suffer an unenviable fate. Eric Shinseki wisely warned, "If you don't like change, you'll like irrelevance even less." My life's mission is to inspire and guide entrepreneurs to create a hopeful, compelling and abundant future for humanity. I've expressed this mission in ten core beliefs within my Abundance360 community:

1. We believe that an entrepreneur's mindset is their greatest asset.

2. We believe that your Massive Transformative Purpose (MTP) can transform an industry and solve a Grand Challenge.

3. We believe every entrepreneur should have a Moonshot they are passionate about implementing, enabled by their MTP.

4. We believe in the power of entrepreneurs to solve the world's biggest problems.

5. We believe it is possible to create wealth while at the same time uplifting humanity.

6. We believe that, by the end of this decade (2030), we will extend the healthy human lifespan by decades.

7. We believe that every organization and entrepreneur must be fully immersed in AI (as soon as possible) to survive and thrive in the decade ahead.

8. We believe that this is the most extraordinary time in human history to be alive.

9. We believe that "the day before something is a break-

through, it's a crazy idea"—so embracing crazy ideas is critical to innovation.

10. We believe that exponential technologies create abundance.

In *The E-Mind*™, Kary doesn't teach us what to think but rather how to think—and how thinking like an entrepreneur gives an exponential advantage in work and life. Regardless of your profession, tapping into the ten Traits that make up The E-Mind will help you navigate our ever-increasing abundant world.

Read this book and apply it. If you do, you'll learn to surf this tsunami of change and survive and thrive.

Remember that this is the most extraordinary time to be alive, a time when entrepreneurs with the right mindset can make their dreams come true and uplift humanity.

Embrace the Future—Don't Fear It.
—Peter H. Diamandis, MD

Serial entrepreneur, futurist, technologist, TED Speaker, New York Times Bestselling Author, founder of Singularity University, The XPRIZE Foundation, and over 20 companies.

Note to You—the Reader

This book is not about cycling.

It's about you and the way you think—the way all successful people think.

I call this "way" The E-Mind.

Rather than give you a book full of research with facts and figures, I decided to tell a story instead. The story includes research, but it's wrapped around a cycling adventure. I believe truth is stickier inside of stories.

You may find the cycling stories helpful, or you may want to skip them. That choice is up to you.

If you're a visual learner like me, then you may also want to "see" the stories with photos and videos. If so, scan the QR code below. When you do, you'll be directed to an album where you can experience the cycling adventure in a deeper way.

Bottom line. Thanks for investing in yourself and your future.

I look forward to our journey together—a journey into The E-Mind.

PART 1

TRIP

Think Like an Entrepreneur

"What do you mean you're canceling?" I asked.

"The other guys and I talked, and we just feel like it wouldn't be right to go to France without Chet."

I paused for a second to keep my emotions in check. "I understand, but I have twelve clients who've already paid for a business workshop. I rented the oldest cafe in Paris six months ago. Everything is set after we cycle the mountains. I can't bail on them, and they've already booked flights and hotels."

"I understand, but you know Chet. He lives for this trip. We can't leave him behind. He's out, so we're out."

I took a deep breath. I couldn't blame them, and I understood their logic, but it didn't take away my disappointment. I'd been training for this cycling trip in the French Alps for more than a year. Chet had invited me many times over the past decade, but quite frankly, the thought scared me too much. I had seen pictures of those mountains. To climb them, I'd have to take my workouts—not to mention my thinking—to a whole different level.

Finally, about a year ago, I said yes. And for the past twelve months, I rode my bike multiple times a week. I disciplined my body and mind, logging thousands and thousands of miles in nearly every weather condition. I maximized my sleeping, eating, and hydration habits and modified them for high performance. You name it, I did it as long as it pushed me closer to my goal—joining my five friends on the adventure of a lifetime.

Now, with one simple phone call, my dream crumbled right before me just six days before departure.

Part of me wanted to bail, too. My friend just handed me a gift-wrapped excuse to cancel the whole trip and avoid the most physically challenging event of my life. Besides, I couldn't craft a new plan in less than a week. But then I thought about my clients. I couldn't let them down. They already booked their travel to Paris. And I bought a four-hour train ticket to join them after cycling the mountains.

My heart was torn in two, and I didn't know what to do.

I contacted the airline. My buddies and I had planned to land in Geneva, Switzerland, rent a car, and drive to Saint Jean de Maurienne, the heart of many of the most grueling cycling routes—often included in the Tour de France. I thought about changing my flight, skipping the mountains, cutting the trip short, and just doing the Paris leg of the trip. After hours and hours on the phone, it boiled down to two choices. I could either keep my flight into Switzerland and go solo to the mountains or pay three times as much for Paris and host my event. Evidently, booking a flight with six days notice jacked up the price.

I understood why Chet backed out. His wife suffered from serious pain for nearly a month, and matters escalated over the past few days. After consulting with an expert, they scheduled immediate surgery. Of course, Chet couldn't go with us to France. He needed to stay and care for his wife. Any compassionate husband would do the same thing.

I didn't fault him. My other friends probably thought they were doing the right thing, too. It *was* Chet's trip, and he had planned everything: the lodging, bike rentals, the sag wagon, even the restaurants. Over the last fifteen years, he and the other guys had cycled in France multiple times. They knew all the tricks—the best place for currency exchange, quick repairs at the local cycling shops, and which mountains to climb and in what order. They mapped out the entire excursion. They told me, the newbie, to trust the process and as long as I'd trained, I would be fine. Boy, had I trained.

Besides, the guys were right. Without Chet, the trip wouldn't be the same. Plus, Dave had canceled six weeks earlier after tearing his shoulder during a workout. Tom, one of the other cyclists in our group, was only recently cleared by his doctor after a concussion and a broken wrist due to a small crash weeks earlier. He was still wearing a wrist brace.

Our perfect plans had been derailed multiple times prior to this phone call, but we'd pressed on. Now, six days before departure, things were beyond worse—worse enough for everyone to bail.

I talked to my wife, Kelly. Part of me felt guilty for still thinking about going. It's one thing to go on a trip to another country with your friends. But, in my mind, it was a whole other thing to go by yourself. It felt selfish. I already felt bad leaving my family to travel. Months before, I decided to do something special for my wife and daughters. I purchased tickets for them to see Taylor Swift in Cincinnati while I was away. I figured if I was in France having a blast, they should also be doing something on their bucket list.

"I think you should go," Kelly said. "You've been training for a long time. And your clients expect you in Paris."

"But those are some of the toughest mountains in the world," I replied. "And I'll be all by myself. Honestly, I don't even know what I'm doing." My excuses flew out of my mouth without even thinking. I guess my fears were getting the best of me. "Besides, I was counting on the other guys to help me figure things out. Plus, there's the language and the rooms and bike rentals have all been canceled. It's just not going to be the same."

"Have you tried calling the airline to get a new ticket straight into Paris?"

"Yeah, but it doesn't make sense to spend even more money for a shorter trip. A new ticket would triple the rate. And flying all that way for a one-day workshop seems foolish."

"Well, I support you and I'm fine with you going," she said.

Kelly always supports me. And a small part of me wanted to go—albeit a very, very small part.

"I'll think about it. I have to make a decision soon—as in the next twenty-four hours."

I sent private messages to a few of my European clients to feel them out. "I'm not sure what to do, Rob and Nicole."

I don't know what I was looking for from them. Maybe an answer? I certainly didn't have one myself. Normally, I'm a very decisive person. But vacillating between two options didn't feel great, and the clock kept ticking.

As a CEO, clearing my calendar for this trip had taken some work. I turned down many opportunities, rescheduled private client meetings, and even paused projects for this once-in-a-lifetime trip.

I knew there were costs and rewards for either decision. I just didn't know what side of the equation I wanted more—regret for not going or risk for going all by myself.

Not My First Solo Ride

A few months ago, I accepted the position to serve as the Berry Chair of Entrepreneurship at Cedarville University in addition to running my two businesses. Eighteen years ago, I felt called to be a professor, and I had applied at that same university, but they rejected me. The timing was obviously wrong. Evidently, the Biblical Studies department didn't think I was the top choice.

I JUST DIDN'T KNOW WHAT SIDE OF THE EQUATION I WANTED MORE—REGRET FOR NOT GOING OR RISK FOR GOING ALL BY MYSELF.

At that time, I was a pastor following in the footsteps of my father, but I knew the church was not my final resting place. I thought a professorship might be, but Cedarville didn't. And so, to satisfy my desire for a creative outlet, I wrote. I enjoyed the written word, and it blended well with my position as a pastor. I published books on multiple topics, and after my fourth, I discovered a unique way to position those books into eighteen streams of income. My books became webinars, workshops, seminars, and keynote speeches.

I stayed in my pastor position for eight years after writing my first book, but my side hustle kept growing. I had never thought of myself as an entrepreneur—just that I wanted to ignite souls. Eventually, the opportunities came faster than I could sustain, and

I had to make a choice. Would I stay comfortable and remain a pastor with a nice salary and benefits, or would I venture out on my own as a full-time entrepreneur?

Leaving the church meant I'd be completely on my own. I'd say goodbye to many friends. No title, no paycheck, and a ton of extra expenses. In addition to my kids' tuition, I'd now be responsible for our health insurance, new taxes, and a hundred other details I had no clue about. Many people advised me to stay at my current job. Why would I want to leave? I had safety, security, and predictability. Why throw it away to go all in as an entrepreneur?

Besides, they told me most entrepreneurs fail, and most businesses go under. Then what? One trusted confidant, I think perhaps even well-meaning, cornered me after a Sunday service. "What makes you think you can go into business? What are you going to sell? What service are you going to provide?"

His questions rifled through me like a soldier shooting bullets from a firing line. I didn't have a good answer, so I didn't bother defending. Who was I fooling? I didn't have a business plan or a product prototype.

I shared my angst with Kelly. Professionally speaking, I'd been settling for quite some time. I was in my thirties with three young kids, and I needed to make a choice.

"I think you should leave," she said, "It's obvious you're not truly happy."

"Yeah, but do you think we can make it?"

"You'll find a way," she said. "I know you'll bring in the money. You have to."

That's my wife. She's practical, and she says it how it is. She didn't give me a flowery speech. She believed in me, but she expected me to provide for her and the kids. Now, I had to look inside, dig deep, and decide if I believed in myself, too.

I chose safety for a season. Why not do both, I reasoned? I could stay a pastor, teach on Sundays, write books, and even speak out of state once in a while. I'd keep my salary and benefits and give a keynote every now and then.

Everything was fine—until one day it wasn't.

Remember that guy Chet? Well, he called me. I had been his kids' youth pastor several years before, and we talked once in a while.

"What's up, Chet?"

"I saw your pictures online," he said, "Looks like you've just got back from a speaking gig about your book. Is the church okay with that?

"Yep, they know about it."

"Is Kelly okay with it?"

"Yeah," I said.

"Is God okay with it?"

"What do you mean?" I asked.

"Listen. I think you're full of !&^%!" Chet had a rare talent for sharing unfiltered truth, often in the form of cuss words.

Dead silence.

"Did you hear me?" he asked calmly.

"You're full of !&^%! I think you're scared, and you're using the church because you don't think you have what it takes. Look at you. You're hiding—telling audiences to live big and bold, and you're living off the church's dime. You can't take the ring and stay in the Shire.

Don't talk to me until you get a spine."

> YOU CAN'T TAKE THE RING AND STAY IN THE SHIRE.

And then nothing.

Dead silence—except for a dial tone.

I couldn't believe it. He hung up on me.

My head was spinning. I needed to vomit.

I had stepped outside to take his call. The warm May day mocked me. I saw blue sky and green grass. Everything was alive and growing—everything except me. I was dying and scared. And my friend had just called me out with jarring words. I felt naked and exposed.

My face flushed red.

I looked around. Who else heard his searing truth?

Nobody except me. But that was enough, and I knew deep inside nothing would ever be the same—and it wasn't. I knew what I needed to do. I'd tell my Senior Pastor the news—after twelve years, I was leaving the pastorate.

The year was 2012, and in that moment of clarity, I made one of the biggest decisions of my life. I stared straight at the entrepreneurial mountain before me, the one I knew I needed to climb. This was a journey I'd have to take all by myself. I had no business background. And although I never traveled this route before, I couldn't hide inside the comfortable church office one day longer. I came clean and set out on the adventure of a lifetime.

Comfortable Climbing Mountains

Leaving the pastorate more than a decade ago was a difficult choice, but I have zero regrets. Entrepreneurship is in my DNA. It's who I was born to be, and it feels natural, though I didn't know it at the time. Don't mistake me. Entrepreneurship hasn't been easy—quite the opposite, actually. It's brought the lowest of lows, including betrayal, failure, and rejection. But it's also brought the highest of highs, including global launches, mind-blowing partnerships, and transformed lives. Through it all, I've never doubted my decision, and I feel more alive than ever.

This past summer, when my friends canceled, I faced a brand new mountain—cycling solo. Would I go, or would I cancel, too?

Similar to the question of changing careers all those years ago, I knew I couldn't let my fears get the best of me. If I didn't go to France, I'd always doubt my decision. The price of regret was far more costly than a little anxiety. Besides, I couldn't disappoint my clients. They paid for the workshop, flights, and lodging. Since I was headed to the country anyway, it made sense to cycle the mountains even though I'd be all alone.

Immediately, I went to YouTube and watched videos about traveling to France. I learned what scams to watch out for, how to pack my bike into a box, and what types of energy bars to bring. The more videos I watched, the more comfortable I felt about boarding the plane and arriving in Switzerland.

My friends Rob and Nicole messaged me back. They explained how to navigate the airport, buy train tickets, and communicate with locals. Despite all their tips, the number one difference maker that helped me navigate the mountains wasn't tangible. It wasn't something you can buy at a store or order online. Rather, it was my mindset, my way of thinking.

Too often, we think something external is going to save us. I meet "wantrepreneurs" every week who buy the equipment, join the community, and watch the videos. But none of these strategies guarantee victory. True success is an internal game. It begins and ends with the way we think.

This is why, before I even boarded the plane to the Alps, I found myself tapping into the same Ten Traits that helped me all of these years in my entrepreneurial journey. I quickly realized the whole trip was a microcosm of what every entrepreneur faces in their business.

In the following pages, you'll encounter a wild European adventure with its fair share of failure and humor. But it's much bigger than that. The real gold you'll discover is how all successful entrepreneurs leverage what I call The E-Mind. This uncommon mindset is essential for achieving better results in life and business.

My hope is that by unpacking the Ten Traits that make up The E-Mind, you'll discover tools to help you climb your own entrepreneurial mountains. These Ten Traits will make your adventure more enjoyable and give you an exponential advantage—regardless of your profession. They've helped me create multiple companies, earn millions of dollars, and, most importantly, change millions of lives around the world. They're the same Ten Traits I now teach to the university students I am blessed to serve.

In keeping with the spirit of cycling and the adventure we're about to take, I visually depict these Ten Traits as ten spokes that make forward progress possible. In each chapter, we'll explore one of the traits in depth. Take away even one of the spokes, and you're in a world of hurt—not to mention a danger to yourself and those around you.

Today's economy and marketplace require every single person to think like an entrepreneur. Those who do will succeed. Those who refuse will not. It's that simple.

So just like Chet called me one day out of the blue armed with searing truth, I'm turning the focus to you and your future. With your permission, I'm going to ask you a simple question. Similar to my choice this past summer, you now have a choice. Will you cancel the trip and sit in the seat of comfortability, or will you go on the adventure of a lifetime?

The plane is about to take off.
You hold the ticket in your hands.
It's time to decide.

PART 2

TRAITS

Trait One: Independence

No One Is Coming to Save You

You're still here. That means you've opted for adventure. You're an outlier and different from most, and for that, I'm proud of you. Congratulations. Together, we'll take a journey deep into the E-Mind.

If you consider yourself an entrepreneur, you're in the minority. According to Gino Wickman, bestselling author and founder of the Entrepreneur Operating System® (EOS®), only 4 percent of the population are true entrepreneurs.[1] Ying Lin puts that number higher at 16.5 percent, at least in the United States among adults. Lin also lists nine other important entrepreneurial statistics:

(1) There are 582 million entrepreneurs in the world.
(2) Nearly 5.1 million new businesses were started in the US in 2022.
(3) As of 2020, there were 274 million female entrepreneurs worldwide.
(4) More than six in ten (63 percent) of US small businesses were profitable in 2020.
(5) 72 percent of US businesses owned by African Americans are profitable.
(6) More than half of the new businesses started in the US over the past decade are minority-owned.
(7) 74.1 percent of adult entrepreneurs in the US say their main motivation for starting a business is to build wealth.
(8) 67.7 percent of the world's wealthiest individuals (with a net worth of at least $30 million) are self-made.

> (9) Nearly one in five (18.7 percent) of businesses worldwide takes on the form of family entrepreneurship in one way or another.[2]

Regardless of the exact number of people who *are* entrepreneurs in the world (somewhere between 4 and 16.5 percent), I believe everybody, i.e., 100 percent of the population, needs to *think* like an entrepreneur. Why, some people may ask. The simple reason is that whether or not we choose to accept the facts, every person on the planet has a personal business and brand.

Author and business management guru Tom Peters wrote a revolutionary article back in 1997 in an issue of *Fast Company* on this topic. In this deeply prophetic piece, Peters explained a future time when everyone would be their own business:

WHETHER OR NOT WE CHOOSE TO ACCEPT THE FACTS, EVERY PERSON ON THE PLANET HAS A PERSONAL BUSINESS AND BRAND.

> Regardless of age, regardless of position, regardless of the business we happen to be in, all of us need to understand the importance of branding. We are CEOs of our own companies: Me Inc. To be in business today, our most important job is to be head marketer for the brand called You.[3]

I've shared this concept with people in my workshops and seminars. The crowd is often split in their response. After examining the evidence, some agree. But many bristle at the thought, believing it to be narcissistic and self-absorbed. Some faith-filled audiences might even think it's anti-Christian.

But, is it?

Jesus taught on the topic of marketing, exhorting his followers to intentionally embody their brand with metaphors like salt and light.

> You are the salt of the earth. But if the salt loses its saltiness, how can it be made salty again? It is no longer good for anything, except to be thrown out and trampled underfoot. You are the light of the world. A town built on a hill cannot be hidden. Neither do people light a lamp and put it under a bowl. Instead they put it on its stand, and it gives light to everyone in the house. In the same way, let your light shine before others, that they may see your good deeds and glorify your Father in heaven.[4]

Jesus warned his disciples not to hide their brand but instead to let it shine for all the world to see. Sadly, I've seen churches and Christians play the humility card rather than taking this branding mandate seriously. Their approach is rooted in laziness and fear. Jesus painted such a person with disdain in his parable of the talents. The one who multiplied their talent was commended. The one who buried it—not so much.

> Then he who had received the one talent came and said, "Lord, I knew you to be a hard man, reaping

> where you have not sown and gathering where you have not scattered seed. And I was afraid, and went and hid your talent in the ground. Look, there you have what is yours." But his lord answered and said to him, "You wicked and lazy servant, you knew that I reap where I have not sown, and gather where I have not scattered seed. So you ought to have deposited my money with the bankers, and at my coming I would have received back my own with interest. So take the talent from him, and give it to him who has ten talents. For to everyone who has, more will be given, and he will have abundance; but from him who does not have, even what he has will be taken away. And cast the unprofitable servant into the outer darkness. There will be weeping and gnashing of teeth."[5]

So what is branding? Sometimes, we overcomplicate the word. When we do, we fail to realize that every single person is a brand, whether they admit it or not. According to *Harvard Business Review*:

> Jeff Bezos, the founder of Amazon, is quoted as saying, "Your brand is what people say about you when you're not in the room." It's the amalgamation of the associations, beliefs, feelings, attitudes, and expectations that people collectively hold about you. Your goal should be to ensure that the narrative created

about you is accurate, coherent, compelling, and differentiated.[6]

Opting Out Is not an Option

Opting out of a personal brand is both naive and impossible for business people and bible people alike. And if we claim to be *both* bible people and business people, then it's twice as ignorant to ignore this truth. Bezos was right. "People are always going to talk about you when you leave the room." Although we can't control the narrative, we certainly can influence it. The Apostle Paul knew this and therefore told his protege Timothy, "Don't let anyone look down on you because you are young, but set an example for the believers in speech, in conduct, in love, in faith and in purity."[7]

Branding starts at an early age and continues until the day we die. We can ignore this truth or embrace it. I tell my university students every time they go for a job interview, the company is deciding if they want to "buy" you, and thus your brand. They check out your social media accounts and dive deep into your personal and professional online presence. For those who claim to be above social media, opting out of it altogether, that decision is also a branding choice as well.

Simply put, "no branding" or "poor branding" is branding too.

Ask any business, and they'll agree—that is, if they're still operational. Too often, inferior branding is the kiss of death to profitability and sustainability.

SIMPLY PUT, "NO BRANDING" OR "POOR BRANDING" IS BRANDING TOO.

We no longer have an excuse for sloppy branding or non-existent branding. Decades ago, maybe so. Today, our mobile phones have evolved into video studios, PR firms, publishers, and global streaming platforms. All these tools have the power to advance your brand. Some people purposely decide not to post anything. Choosing not to engage speaks as loudly as daily memes, maybe even louder.

The Catholic church, one of the oldest enterprises in existence today, acknowledges this truth rather than ignores it. Someone in power made the decision to create social media accounts for the Pope, and the Catholic brand reaches millions worldwide every single day.

Looks like Tom Peters was right before social media was even a thing. He taught us back in 1997:

> You're every bit as much a brand as Nike®, Coke®, Pepsi®. To start thinking like your own favorite brand manager, ask yourself the same question the brand managers at Nike, Coke, Pepsi, ask themselves: What is it that my product or service does that makes it different.[8]

Hopefully, you're starting to see that—whether you like it or not—you're both a business and a brand. Take courage, this doesn't mean you need to become an expert at social media if it doesn't make sense or if you hate it. If branding isn't your thing, you can always delegate the task and find a Who instead. In the words of my coach, Dan Sullivan, co-founder of Strategic Coach® and creator of the WhoNotHow® concept, "When you want to accomplish something, stop asking, 'How can I do this?' ...instead, 'Who can do this for me?'"[9] This question is at the heart of the WhoNotHow philosophy.

Defining Entrepreneurship

> Before we go any further, we'd do well to define an entrepreneur. In one sense, the word literally means one who bears risk. In another sense, according to Shopify, an entrepreneur is: Someone who has an idea and who works to create a product or service that people will buy, as well as an organization to support that effort. An entrepreneur takes on most of the risk and initiative for their new business and is often seen as a visionary or innovator.[10]

If you don't think of yourself as a "real" entrepreneur—whatever that actually means—don't worry. Maybe you're hard-wired to be an *intrapreneur* instead. That's great news for anyone who doesn't want to start or own their own business! We need plenty of intrapreneurs.

So what is an intrapreneur? Great question. Here are three definitions:

1. Intrapreneurs are employees of a company who are assigned to work on a special idea or project. They are given the time and freedom to develop the project as an entrepreneur would. However, they are not working solo. Intrapreneurs have the resources and capabilities of the firm at their disposal.[11]

2. Intrapreneurs are individuals who are tasked with creating new and innovative products within an already-established business. Backed by a company's available resources, intrapreneurs develop open-ended ideas and turn them into real-world products and services.[12]

3. Intrapreneurs are employees with entrepreneurial skills who are responsible for developing innovative ideas, products, or services for their company. Their goal is to enhance the sustainability of the business and help it stay ahead of the competition. Intrapreneurs are not directly held responsible for the success or failure of the experiments they do. They neither receive any credit individually for the success nor do they get blamed for the failure.[13]

The point of this book is not to turn you into an entrepreneur or even an intrapreneur, for that matter. Rather, it's to give you Ten Traits to help you think like an entrepreneur and gain an exponential advantage. When you leverage these Ten Traits, regardless of your role inside or outside of a company, you'll experience even more success. This is because thinking like an entrepreneur is essential. The continual shifts in technology demand it.

In my bestselling book *Unhackable*, I reveal how knowledge used to double every thousand years. According to IBM, today it doubles every twelve hours![14] This means change is inevitable—whether we ignore it or invite it. Choosing to stay the same is the biggest risk of all. If we want to remain relevant, we must grow and adapt. Choosing ignorance means irrelevance is right around the corner.

Eric Hoffer says it clear, concise, and direct, "In times of change, learners inherit the earth, while the learned find themselves beautifully equipped to deal with a world that no longer exists."[15]

IF WE WANT TO REMAIN RELEVANT, WE MUST GROW AND ADAPT. CHOOSING IGNORANCE MEANS IRRELEVANCE IS RIGHT AROUND THE CORNER.

Playing the Game of Entrepreneurship

Personally, I love change. I'm bored by routine and predictability. Maybe you can relate? As a way to fight it, I invite novelty and unpredictability—even in the food choices I make.

I love risk, and I enjoy the game—knowing I have an opportunity to win and lose every single day. If you're like me and you crave flow, the optimal state of human performance, that means you need a real chance of failure built into your life. If not, you'll coast on autopilot and drift toward disengagement. This is why many people seek out vacations. They intentionally invite a pattern interruption that wakes them back up.

Many years ago, back in my day job, I was drifting toward disengagement. As a pastor, I enjoyed much of my role. However, working inside a church wasn't exactly new or novel. Don't get me wrong. I believe pastoral work is significant. I influenced people and perhaps even their eternities a few times. That work is incredibly exciting. However, it was the endless meetings every day, often about trivial matters, that threatened to kill my creativity.

When I became an entrepreneur, the stakes rose exponentially. If I didn't bring home clients, I didn't bring home food. Without deals or new product launches, I couldn't pay for health insurance. Not many people like that kind of pressure. In fact, most people hate it because it causes stress. For some reason, I revel in the pressure.

When I decided to go to France without my friends, I felt immediate stress, and much like my initial reaction to entrepreneurship, I didn't think I could make it. Instead of seeing the opportunities, I only envisioned the insurmountable mountains awaiting me—literal mountains, in this case. Endless details flooded my mind. I'd never been to Switzerland.

> Could I ship my bike without it breaking?
> What kind of gear would I need for the mountain tops covered in snow?
> Would they be covered in snow, or would it have melted by June?

> What if I ran out of water or got lost or rode off the road and crashed?

The pressure mounted, as did the need to find a room in some random mountainside town, with a name I couldn't pronounce. The stress kept coming, especially regarding the language barrier inside the Airbnb app I used to communicate with a potential host. Finding food as I cycled would be a challenge, too.

> Did stores carry cycling gels, salt tablets, and electrolyte powders?
> Where would I convert my US dollars into francs?
> Wait. Did they use francs or euros?

The unknowns kept coming, without any clear answers. The stakes were high, and everyone who was supposed to help me through the questions bailed. No one was coming to save me.

The thing about entrepreneurs is that many times, we're walking paradoxes. We love high stakes and challenges, but we also hate high stakes and challenges—until we overcome them. Then we get a rush and crave even bigger challenges. We keep leveling-up and growing our confidence and competence. That's the beauty of being an entrepreneur. It's also the beauty of the E-Minds—those outliers who embrace *different*, especially regarding their thinking.

By going it alone, you face your fears head on. You realize it's all on you—the success and the failure. This is why I depended so much upon God. On those literal and figurative mountains, most of the time, I didn't have anyone else to rely on.

When you're all alone cycling up multiple mountain passes for eleven hours a day, you do a ton of internal work. You can't run or hide and distracting yourself could mean riding off a cliff to your death. For real. Success demands an engaged mind and an active heart. Focus isn't optional and victory isn't guaranteed. This is what makes the game so fun.

SUCCESS DEMANDS AN ENGAGED MIND AND AN ACTIVE HEART.

My guess is that you can relate—at least on this level. Reflect back to who you were as a child. On a daily basis you went off script and made everything up. Thinking like an entrepreneur is a return to your childhood. It's fun and unpredictable and the adventure of a lifetime, much like learning how to ride a bicycle.

Just like every bike needs two wheels, every successful person needs these Ten Traits. This is because the game of life has changed—whether you want to admit it or not. The truth is people no longer stay in one job for decades. In fact, your next places of employment may not even exist at the moment.

> Today we're all bearers of risk.
> Will Social Security be around when we retire?
> Will the US dollar be here in twenty years or will we all be using cryptocurrency?
> What if most jobs move to the metaverse or there's

another lockdown?
What if your employer shuts the doors?

The unknowns of our last decade far outweigh those from any other time in human history. No one is immune, and everyone is vulnerable. We think we have guarantees, but now we know better.

The Danger of Depending too Much on Others

One day in France, I had no clue how to order my meal at a unique restaurant that included a line. I turned to the person behind me and I saw an older lady. I said bonjour and tried asking for help in English. To my surprise, she replied in English. She graciously guided me through ordering my salmon. After I paid for my lunch and searched a bit, I found a table with two seats. A couple of minutes later, the woman asked if she could sit with me.

We chatted in between bites and I learned she was visiting from Austria. I marveled as she told me how her government provided for many of its citizens' needs—from health care to education. But rather than happiness, I sensed a heaviness in her voice. She went on to tell me about her deep fear regarding the Austrian Social Security System. In her mind, all that government provision created a dangerous dependency. Many people in her country no longer knew how to care for themselves. This growing reliance fed some precarious conditions.

I could see her point. Then I reflected upon my own country. Compared to Austria, the United States aligns much more with the E-Mind. At least historically speaking, my government isn't going to save its citizens. If entrepreneurs create a faulty product, a poor business model, or an unpopular service, they will fail. The marketplace chews you up and spits you out. For better or worse, success and failure begins and ends with entrepreneurs.

When I left the safety of the church as a pastor and became a full-time entrepreneur, I knew I could never go back. There was no parachute and no one would save me. My wife Kelly knew it, too, and that's why she told me I needed to find a way. I did what Tony Robbins calls, "burning the ships." And it's the same strategy the prophet Elisha implemented when he burned his plowing equipment thousands of years ago after deciding to exchange the life of a farmer for one of a prophet. Going all in commits us in ways we never thought possible. By showing up filled up, we experience a different kind of energy.

I immediately saw entrepreneurial parallels to my cycling trip in France. On those mountains, I made a few calls back to the States. When I talked to Chet, he wanted to know how I was doing. I told him I was having the time of my life climbing all of these mountains all by myself.

"Look, if you get too tired, you can always call a cab or order an Uber or a Lyft," he said, trying to encourage me.

"I have no idea how to get a cab in this country," I laughed. "And these small French towns don't have Ubers or Lyfts. I already asked the locals."

He grew quiet for a moment, feeling the weight of my aloneness. When he came to France on past trips, he had a rental car or someone driving a sag wagon. In case of an injury, they had backup. When they got tired, the vehicle picked them up. If one of them had a problem with a bike, the sag wagon drove to their rescue. They had water, supplies, and assistance only a quick phone call away. In other words, when Chet cycled France, he was never alone.

No shame or blame and I didn't mind the pressure. In fact, I started liking the solo component. Each day I planned out potential routes. Then I calculated how many mountains I could climb and still make it back before daylight. I didn't always judge correctly. (More on that later.) I had to estimate my water and food, and hope for a refueling station somewhere along the way. I packed a credit card, (falsely) assuming every store would accept plastic.

I came to terms with the reality that no one was coming to save me. Adopting this mindset ensured success came faster and easier.

I woke each day based upon the respective train departure times that would transport my bicycle and me to far away towns with roads that led to even higher mountain peaks. Sometimes the trains came. Other times, they were delayed or rerouted. I filled my small saddle pack with an extra innertube, a CO2 cartridge, and tire repair kit in case I encountered a flat. I fully embraced Independence, the first Trait of The E-Mind.

It's the same trait I leveraged when I left the pastorate. Back then, I quickly learned what it took to create a new corporation with the state of Ohio. People told me to separate my personal assets from my business assets. I mastered new terms like S Corp, C Corp, LLC, sole proprietorship, and partnership.

To be successful on this solo cycling trip, I quickly realized I needed to tap into that same E-Mind thinking. I soon mastered new terms like Category 2 and Category 1 climbs. And by accident, I even learned the meaning of HC or "Hors Category." Evidently, a few of the mountains Chet told me to climb were categorized as HC, meaning the climb is above categorization. They're steep, long, and brutal.[16]

The truth is that if you want to make it cycling solo in France or conducting business solo anywhere in the world, then you need to adapt the mindset that no one is coming to your rescue. This doesn't mean success is gained by rugged individualism. Hardly. People, connections, and networks matter. The myth of the self-made person is just that—a myth. But if you're dependent upon others to do the work for you, then you're going to be in a world of hurt. And this is the exact reason why much of our planet is in a world of hurt. We act like victims, rather than victors.

Lying in BED or using your OAR

Two of my most favorite acronyms demonstrate the drastic difference between victims and victors.

Victims lie in BED—blame, excuses, and denial. Victors, on the other hand, use their OAR to keep moving forward——ownership, accountability, and responsibility. Victims believe the world happens to *them*. Victors believe *they* happen to the world. Here's the difference, stacked side by side.

Victims	**Victors**
The world happens to them.	*They happen to the world.*
Blame	Ownership
Excuses	Accountability
Denial	Responsibility

Many times in my entrepreneurial journey—or my French cycling journey for that matter—I revisited this chart.

I had to ask:

- Am I being a victim in this situation?
- Am I lying in BED?
- Am I blaming circumstances, making excuses, and living in denial?

OR

- Am I choosing to be a victor in this situation?
- Am I putting OAR in the water and advancing?
- Am I taking ownership, accountability, and responsibility for my results?

This is the power of the E-Mind. It makes no difference whether you're in sports, medicine, education, or at the grocery store trying to find something out of stock. This mindset will help you navigate more effectively and efficiently.

Every day, in every situation, we can choose to think like victims or victors. Many times, we hop back and forth between the two—even on the same day.

I know I do.

I might crush it in a business meeting and close gaps. Then I might literally make excuses for why I forgot to bring home milk when I was out and about. It can happen that quickly.

Life has a funny way of exposing our thinking. If we're not careful, we tend to give away our power. When circumstances are amazing it's easy to become prideful and think we're the cause.

Then if conditions change and we face adversity, we can slip into blaming other people or things. But neither extreme is healthy. Circumstances don't ruin us—they simply reveal us. We're the ones who choose our attitude and mindset.

CIRCUMSTANCES DON'T RUIN US—THEY SIMPLY REVEAL US.

Approaching Life as an Adventure

Bottom line. We have one of two choices. We can either live as victims and believe God is *against* us. Or we can live as victors and believe God is *for* us. The choice we make, makes us. This is my approach to life. And it's the same approach I used on my France trip. When all my buddies were bailing, I could have assumed this trip wasn't God's will. That would have been easier to swallow.

All the external circumstances could have easily convinced me I shouldn't go to the Alps. After all, look at the signs:

- Dave tore his shoulder.
- Tom crashed a couple of weeks prior and suffered a concussion and a broken wrist.
- Chet's wife needed immediate surgery.
- Mike's wife experienced a health scare.

Part of me felt like the trip was cursed and that I shouldn't go either. But then I thought about the flipside. Maybe God wanted to teach me something on the trip. Maybe God wanted me to trust him in a bigger way. I certainly didn't plan on getting the inspiration for this book while I was cycling alone on the mountains.

Or maybe the whole reason I went had nothing to do with me. Maybe it was for you—to prepare you for your great entrepreneurial adventure! Maybe this book needed to happen because you needed to learn how to think like an entrepreneur and gain an exponential advantage. Maybe your future idea or business is going to change the world—or at least *someone's* world.

A long time ago I decided to see everything as a gift—even the disappointments of life. I don't always get it perfectly. But I borrowed this perspective from Albert Einstein who said, "There are two ways to live: you can live as if nothing is a miracle; you can live as if everything is a miracle."[17] This is easy to say, yet hard to do. Of course, many

MAYBE YOUR FUTURE IDEA OR BUSINESS IS GOING TO CHANGE THE WORLD— OR AT LEAST SOMEONE'S WORLD.

circumstances in life are deep and painful. And yet, I believe Anaïs Nin was onto something when she wrote, "We don't see things as they are, but as we are." It's our perspective that brings meaning to life.

This doesn't mean we pretend life is always perfect. Adversity is a reality, but it makes some people bitter and other people better. The real issue isn't adversity but what we do with it.

I think some people give God too much credit for adversity. Hear me out now before you think I'm a heretic. When facing a mountain, sometimes we're unsure what step to take. We lack faith. This "lack" fuels us, kicking our imagination into overdrive. We rationalize, "Well maybe this is a sign God doesn't want me to do X, Y, or Z." We let this fear keep us frozen and we tell ourselves—and everyone else—that we're waiting on God. The truth is, maybe God is waiting on us to act.

I prefer the opposite approach. When I find myself in trying times where I lack faith, I tell myself that maybe God wants to stretch me because I'm being prepared for a bigger assignment.

Look at all the people in the Bible. Many faced serious adversity, but they took action nonetheless. Some of them did some pretty extraordinary things in the process—like build an ark, kill a giant, and cross the Red Sea. These actions seem bizarre when you think about it, but each action required faith and risk. Rather than putting blame *on* God, they demonstrated faith *in* God. Only recently I realized how each one of these people thought like entrepreneurs. The Bible positions their risk in a favorable light. "Without faith, it is impossible to please God."[18]

From this verse it seems like God is actually pleased by the entrepreneurial mindset, the person who takes him at his word, the one who acts and takes risks. But let's take it one step further. Maybe God was actually the first entrepreneur. (Remember the definition of an entrepreneur: one who bears risk.)

Think about it.

God had the perfect life—no sin, no humans to rescue, no angels to rebel. The Trinity was safe. But maybe God took a huge "risk" creating the world and an even bigger risk giving his creation an option to choose obedience or disobedience.[19] Would we eat from that tasty looking tree or reject the forbidden fruit? The stakes were high. The risk was deep.

We might as well face the truth. Risk is part of life. Everything else is an illusion.

And so as we tie a bow with this first Trait I want to compliment you. After all, you took a big risk. You picked up this book. You could have bailed on the E-Mind just like I could have bailed on the cycling trip. Yet you didn't. And for this reason, I'm proud of you. Rather than running from adventure you signed up for an even bigger one.

Your reward is coming. Trait number one gives you an edge. Independence means no one is coming to save you. And the quicker you accept that, the sooner you can own success in a bigger way. When you shed your dependence upon other people and external factors, you remove blame, excuses, and denial. In its place you develop the internal confidence of a secret weapon—the E-Mind.

Those who turn back remember the ordeal.
Those who persevere remember the adventure.
—Milo Arnold

Trait Two: Flexibility

Map It Out, Then Make It Up.

I grew up in the nineteen eighties.

One of my favorite TV shows back then was the A-Team. Maybe you were alive to remember the storyline? If not, I'd love the honor of introducing you.

To summarize, the producers designed each episode around the same plot. The four main characters—Faceman, Murdock, Mr. T. and "Hannibal"—always got caught up in some kind of trouble. Then they'd put their heads together and solve the problem. By the end of the episode, chock full of over-the-top action scenes, they emerged successful. "Hannibal" concluded the show with his favorite catch phrase, "I love it when a plan comes together."

If you missed it, you didn't miss much. You can watch a single episode on YouTube and then consider yourself an "A-Team" expert. It's predictable and formulaic.

For entrepreneurs, it's the complete opposite. The journey is neither predictable nor formulaic. We plan, but the plan always changes. This is why E-Minds stay flexible.

Someone once said, "Blessed are the flexible for they shall not break." That person must have been an entrepreneur. Make no mistake, being flexible doesn't mean you skip the planning. Like much of entrepreneurship, it's a paradox.

WE PLAN, BUT THE PLAN ALWAYS CHANGES. THIS IS WHY E-MINDS STAY FLEXIBLE.

Go slow to go fast.

Get clarity to step into ambiguity.

Map it out. Then make it up.

Map it Out

In the final hours leading up to France, I went into planner mode. I carefully mapped out my itinerary. I'd leave Columbus at 2:45 PM then land in Washington for a departure at 5:20 PM. After an 8 hour and 20 minute flight I'd land in Geneva, Switzerland before 7:40 AM GVA. An early arrival meant I could get through customs easily, find a cab, then take a train to St. Jean de Maurienne. From there I would check into my Airbnb, reassemble my bicycle, head out into beautiful sunshine, and make it to the top of Col de la Madeleine by afternoon. The first day in France would be a perfect, precise day of fun and adventure.

Or so I planned.

The reality was quite a different experience. Everything went according to plan until we boarded the flight to Switzerland. As expected, high-priced first-class seats are in great demand on an overseas flight. Who wouldn't want a chair that converts into a bed? But when three of the seat belts didn't work, the repair crew boarded the plane and tried for over an hour to fix them.

No luck.

The attendants spent another hour trying to coax three people in first class to downgrade to the mid level seats. Finally, they obliged and we took off two hours behind schedule.

Because we landed in Geneva so late, the customs department was overwhelmed by the other flights that actually arrived on time. I found myself in a thick sea of people waiting for the understaffed customs stations to verify and then stamp our passports. Nearly two hours later, I finally made it through customs.

While standing in line I realized my train ticket would now be wasted. At this late hour, I couldn't get a refund, so I quickly booked another ticket for four hours after my original one. I assumed I could find my luggage, hail a cab, and get to the train station in that amount of time.

Stay flexible, right?

Sounds simple

But first, I had to find my massive bike box. Since my friends bailed, we all opted for a partial refund for the rental bikes. (We canceled so close to our actual trip that we lost the ability for a full refund.) Besides, I didn't understand the whole process of getting the bikes and dropping them off when I finished, so I decided to bring mine instead. Less complicated, I thought. With a little research, I discovered my airline counted a bike box as a luggage piece. It seemed easy enough, so Chet let me borrow an old bike box.

Thanks to YouTube, I learned how to break my bike down into small pieces—springs, screws, pedals, handlebar, derailleur, seat, and more. I took pictures with my smartphone during each step of the process so I'd know how to reassemble the bike upon arrival overseas.

Sleep deprived from the inability to doze off on the plane, I wandered groggily through the baggage claim area trying to ask for help—not an easy thing to do when the workers only speak French. My Google Translate app offered assistance, but needless to say, the process was far from smooth. After fifteen minutes of searching the baggage claim area, I finally found my box in a special area for oversized baggage. Although this bike box had two small wheels on the bottom, it was measured over 5 feet tall and nearly 3 feet wide.

I set out to find a taxi, dragging the bike box behind me. I didn't care what type of vehicle it was, I just needed to make my train or I'd burn another ticket and have to wait another four hours for the next one. The language barrier made it a bit challenging. I wheeled my suitcase with one arm and my bike box with the other. I also carried a backpack with my laptop and personal items inside.

I asked a woman for help locating a cab. With broken English and hand signals, I finally found a taxi. I showed him the address to the train station on my phone and made an effort to figure out how much the ride would cost me. He abruptly waved me inside and told me he'd figure it out when we got there.

One of the YouTube videos I watched in prep for France had warned me about this kind of scam. The woman in the video advised that I should agree on an exact price before I got in any vehicle. However, I didn't have the time nor the language skills to argue, so I simply said, "Go." As we drove, I asked again about the cost, but I was scolded this time. I only had US dollars in my wallet, so I hoped we'd work it out somehow.

My plan disintegrated even further, but it's a good thing I had flexibility on my side.

We rushed through the streets of Geneva, and after a seven-minute drive, he told me the fare would be fifty-five US dollars. I knew this was exorbitant, but I had little choice. I just thanked him, retrieved my bags,

MY PLAN DISINTEGRATED EVEN FURTHER, BUT IT'S A GOOD THING I HAD FLEXIBILITY ON MY SIDE.

and sprinted to the station entrance, realizing I now only had a few minutes to find my train.

The hustle and bustle injected another shot of anxiety into my already amped body. Still pivoting at every turn, I knew I'd find a way. I asked one man for help with no success. I quickly turned to another couple who couldn't produce a quick answer. The minutes vanished and the angst grew. Finally, a different gentleman sensing my panic, swooped in and offered help. He took my phone, internalized the information, and then pointed to a ramp.

"Hurry," he said with a thick accent. "Train leaving."

I sprinted up the ramp, dragging my bike box, suitcase, and backpack. Completely out of breath, I showed my phone to the train worker. He shook his head up and down and I let out a deep sigh. I stood there in front of the train waiting for it to open. I had arrived with one minute to spare.

After thirty seconds of absolutely nothing, the train worker reached out and punched the button on the train. "Push," the gentleman said. I heard a few locals laugh at the American unaccustomed to such cultural nuances.

More thankful than embarrassed, I stepped inside and the train door slammed behind me. Less than thirty seconds later the train jolted forward. Good thing that man pushed the button for me. If he hadn't, I would have stood there waiting. Then I would have watched it speed away and wonder why.

I quickly shoved my luggage away from the sliding door. Immediately, a man standing at the threshold, shushed me. He wasn't about to let his baby wake up. I contemplated where to put my cumbersome bike box. The new father motioned for me to leave it in the doorway of the train. Then he pointed adamantly to the next train car.

Sleep deprivation took its toll and I struggled to process all the stimuli, not to mention the foreign language. Finally, I interpreted his advice and shuffled to the next car. Fueled by adrenaline up until this point, I was beyond tired. Still, I felt a great deal of relief, knowing the train barreled toward France. I smiled at the people around and a kind couple nearby made small talk in broken English.

As the train pushed through Geneva and the countryside of France, I crafted a new plan. After the three-hour train ride, I'd hop on a bus to St. Jean de Maurienne and then somehow find my rental apartment.

When the train finally stopped, I saw the man with the baby who was now awake. The kind father led me to the ascenseur (elevator). After a quick ride down, he guided me up a ramp to the main street. With our translation app, he told me he could take me no further, but pointed down a road and said I'd find the bus somewhere in that direction. I sincerely thanked him for his help.

By this time, I had to use the restroom, but didn't know where to find one. The nearby police officers pointed one out and I dragged my bike box and suitcase inside. At this point, I knew I needed a currency exchange, but again, I had no clue where to find one. Every single need I had required a question and therefore a person who could provide an answer. I felt helpless, but the kind people all around jumped in to provide assistance.

I set out down the street, looking for my bus, dragging my luggage behind me.

Make It Up

Flexibility became the motto for my entire journey. Of course, I didn't just show up in a foreign country without a plan. But although I had made one, without any doing of my own, that plan quickly lost relevance. Timelines faded. Details changed. But in the end, my mindset mattered the most. I held on to the fact that the only thing I could control was myself.

I could've succumbed to a bad attitude or anxiety-infused panic. Instead, I simply tapped into the E-Mind. Comparing my French experience to my entrepreneurial journey, I realized both shared a common thread. Each demanded a plan, but each also required flexibility. In both settings, I mapped it out, but then I made it up.

Here's what I mean.

When I left the church and entered the world of entrepreneurship, of course, I had a very loose plan. Little did I know, my plans, just like my French itinerary, would change by the minute. Good thing I stayed flexible. Circumstances and conditions shifted on a daily basis.

Like one day, many years ago, we had a huge webinar planned. We invested over $50,000 into ads for this particular webinar. These ads worked and thousands of people registered for the big day. We had done this many times throughout the years, so it was no big deal. Although we started smaller with a smaller $1000 ad spend, over time, we scaled it 50x and it worked beautifully.

I'd teach the attendees all about becoming an author and how to turn their books into eighteen streams of income. At the end of the webinar, if they loved the content, we invited them to apply to become published authors. Although hundreds applied, we only accepted the best fifty authors into our class. These authors went on to write life-changing books. The experience was quite fulfilling and we rinsed and repeated this process every 6–8 weeks for about five years.

But that particular day, we encountered a problem—a scenario we didn't account for. On the morning of the webinar, I awoke with a sore throat. It was worse than that. I had no voice—at best, I could whisper. It would be impossible to give an inspirational and educational two-hour webinar. We had mapped it out using the same path we'd traveled many times before, but this time, we had to make it up—and fast.

I quickly wrote an email to all the attendees explaining the situation. I told them how I'd show up live in a few hours, wave to them, and then start a recording of a past webinar. I knew attendance would drop off significantly if I simply showed a recording with no explanation. We knew the stats about recorded webinars used by our competitors. Based upon our research, attendees were much more attentive during live presentations. Understandably, they were turned off by instructors who lied and fooled them into "evergreen" webinars, which simply streamed recordings. Our competitors used that technology and it backfired.

In my email, I told my attendees I literally couldn't speak. However, I also told them I'd sit with them the entire webinar and type in comments during the recording. I'd keep my camera on in the corner of the screen so they could see me. I told them to test me by typing their name into the comment box. I promised to respond to their comments in real time, even addressing them by name so they knew it was a live webinar. I also told them I'd stay on after and type out answers to all their questions.

My strategy worked, although I "made it up" on the spot. The attendees felt my authenticity and the show-up rate was even better than normal. The engagement rate was off the charts too because they wanted to see if I'd actually stay until the end. That day—the day I lost my voice—went down as one of our best webinars ever. Many authors applied, and we quadrupled our investment.

Another time, on a different webinar, just one hour before I was scheduled to go live, the power went out—no lights, no heat, and worse yet, no internet. I felt the anxiety rising within me. I knew our young business couldn't survive if we had to flush $50,000 in ad spend down the drain. I remembered that E-Minds don't focus on obstacles. So I shifted my focus to opportunities.

THAT DAY—THE DAY I LOST MY VOICE—WENT DOWN AS ONE OF OUR BEST WEBINARS EVER.

"What COULD I do instead?"

One option emerged rather quickly. I ditched my original "map" and made up a new one on the spot. I drove to my wife's office ten minutes down the road. Since she's a therapist with counseling clients, I knew I couldn't go inside and bother her. I pivoted, connecting to her wifi, then I proceeded to host the webinar from my car. I didn't want the noise of a coffee shop drowning out my passion, so I chose the intimacy of my car. I told the attendees the truth and didn't worry about their response.

Some attendees might have thought, "Why is this supposedly 'successful guy' doing a webinar from his car? Can't he afford an office?" I didn't worry about their potential opinions. Instead, I focused on providing true value.

Retreat Is Not an Option

Back in France, after several failed attempts, I finally found the right bus and rode it all the way to Saint Jean de Maurienne. Unfortunately, when I arrived, I had no idea how to get to my Airbnb. Although I had a phone with maps, there was no Lyft or Uber in this small mountain town. Maybe a cab would work, but I didn't know how to find one. Overly tired and unable to speak the language, I wanted to get to my destination and crash, so I decided to just start walking.

Backpack over my shoulder, I dragged a suitcase with one arm and my bike box with the other. After walking multiple blocks, I showed a few young boys the address on my phone. Only able to speak French, their hand gestures led me to believe I was heading in the right direction, I kept on walking. The narrow sidewalks prevented me from dragging my luggage side-by-side so I walked down the middle of the road instead.

I came here to cycle in the mountains, and St. Jean de Maurienne didn't disappoint—boasting steep inclines all around. My apartment proved much further than I guessed and it was uphill the whole way. Google Maps bounced around, pointing me in one direction and then another. In the midst of all the rerouting, I just started laughing. What else could I do?

The more I thought about how I must look and the complete collapse of my carefully planned itinerary, the more I laughed. A script writer couldn't have dreamt up something this hilarious.

Quitting didn't even register. Where would I go? Besides, I'd already committed to Trait Number One—Independence. No one was coming to save me. Who was I going to call? I had positioned myself in a place where retreat was not an option. Even though the scenario didn't look anything like my original plan, it's exactly what I signed up for.

THE MORE I THOUGHT ABOUT HOW I MUST LOOK AND THE COMPLETE COLLAPSE OF MY CAREFULLY PLANNED ITINERARY, THE MORE I LAUGHED.

Trait Number Two—Flexibility—has served me well in my entrepreneurial journeys. Late 2019 was simply another example.

Our business grew rapidly, as did our annual Fall Igniting Souls Conference. We had a record turnout with a record profit. As 2019 winded down, I pre-paid $80,000 to the hotel to save on taxes that year. This seemed wise at the time, but unfortunately, 2020 brought with it an unplanned event. The global pandemic forced the hotel into shutdown mode due to COVID protocol. They closed their doors against both our wishes. Plans changed without any warning.

Our small business couldn't sustain this type of unforeseen event. But what could we do? Entrepreneurs stay flexible, that's what we do. We mapped it out, but then new events invited us to make it up. As a result, we decided to host an online summit right in the middle of COVID that Spring. We granted a FREE ticket to anyone and everyone. We made a decision to give, not to get. This gesture of goodwill stuck with our clients throughout the summer. They remained engaged and supportive, albeit from across states and countries. That Fall, we hosted our first-ever Igniting Souls Conference hybrid style, broadcasting it to every continent minus Antarctica. We ignited souls around the world, and the hotel graciously allowed us to spend our deposit over the next two years.

Our flexibility paid off and we navigated a major storm that could have sunk our ship.

Remember, even if you're not an entrepreneur, adopting the E-Mind serves you well. As you already know, life doesn't come with guarantees. The truth is we all benefit from staying flexible. Whether or not you start your own business, thinking like an entrepreneur gives you an exponential advantage. We might as well welcome chaos and stay flexible, because it's all part of the game.

Flexibility Makes Room for Flow

Consider the opposite—inflexibility. Many corporate cultures and institutions boast about being static, dogmatic, and unchanging. On the surface, this may appear like a position of strength, but it's actually rooted in weakness and fear. Without flexibility we can't grow, but we also can't get into flow.

In my book, *Unhackable,* I share Captain Sullivan's story. For nearly three decades, the pilot followed courses mapped out for him, but on January 15, 2009, he had to make it up—and he only had seconds to do so. Even though Captain Sully worked within the very inflexible culture of commercial airlines, he thought like an entrepreneur. And because he did, he successfully landed a plane on the Hudson River and saved every person on that plane.

The world couldn't believe it. Some called it a miracle. But this time, the miraculous had some assistance. Captain Sully flew glider planes on the side. As a result, he naturally adopted the second trait from the E-Mind—Flexibility. He knew how to map it out and then make it up.

No one had written a protocol to land a plane in the Hudson. Sully had to make it up on the spot—with tower control shouting out distracting and unhelpful comments. He had already embraced Trait One—Independence. He knew no one was coming to save him. But then Sully tapped into flow—the optimal state of human performance. He allowed his experience and training to take over, by thinking like an entrepreneur.

Flexibility and flow are a regular part of my entrepreneurial life. Sometimes technology works. Sometimes it doesn't. Sometimes ads work. Sometimes they don't. Most vendors work well. But a few don't and they go out of business. Then we need to map it out and make it up—all over again. Life is fluid and we need to be too.

By staying flexible and in flow, new options open up. This isn't theory, it's neuroscience. Lateral pattern recognition is a byproduct. By staying flexible, we can connect the dots regarding disparate information, facts, and figures—just like Sully. In flow, our prefrontal cortex goes dim, and so does our inner critic, a phenomenon called transient hypofrontality. By staying flexible and in flow, we create new, novel ideas.[20]

In my business ventures, I've experienced quite a few detours. COVID snuck up on us—and everyone else in the world. This pandemic threatened our annual conference, so we chose flexibility and transitioned to a hybrid event instead.

Another time we received a cease-and-desist letter from The Academy of Motion Picture Arts and Sciences. Evidently they heard about our author event—the Author Academy Awards, named after our publishing company Author Academy Elite. They told us we needed to change the name immediately, claiming it created confusion with the Oscar® trademark. After several conversations we realized it wasn't worth a legal battle. Guess what? We stayed flexible and changed our name to Author Elite Awards.

Another time, a "friend" intentionally bought a domain address named after our company. Then he blackmailed us for thousands of dollars and offered to sell it to us. We could have dug in and fought or sued him. Instead, we paid him his fee and received the domain name. Other options would've taken us away from our mission and created sideways energy.

This doesn't mean you never dig in your heels. Once in a while, you may have to make that choice. Just know that people will betray you, steal from you, and create competitive companies. I've experienced all three scenarios. This is what entrepreneurs sign up for. The only way you make it through is to face it head on. As Marcus Aurelius eloquently stated thousands of years ago, "What stands in the way becomes the way."

In other words, map it out and then make it up.

I finally arrived at my Airbnb in St. Jean de Maurienne. Trying to communicate with the apartment owner in French was another adventure altogether. But, instead of riding on my first day as planned, I avoided the rain, stayed inside, and rebuilt my bike. Then after an hour or so, I walked to the grocery store.

After struggling with the labels trying to discern different products, I settled on smoked salmon, bottled water, cheese, yogurt, avocados, dates, and dark chocolate with pistachios. I went back to my Airbnb, ate one of everything and then mapped out the routes for my new day one.

Despite my best plans today, tomorrow would bring a new set of challenges. I chose to stay flexible because I may have to make it up all over again—just like I did today. But I didn't worry or stress. Thanks to the E-Mind I knew I'd find a way through.

The Obstacle is the Way

—Ryan Holiday

Trait Three: Risk

Embarrassment Is Your Ally

I enjoy surprising my university students.

During one particular lecture, I asked them if they were ready for a deep thought. When they nodded their heads, I dropped the truth bomb. Ready for it?

Babies don't blush.

They just stared at me, wondering if I was joking. But I wasn't joking. I just stayed silent, letting the thought sink in. I had imagined this deep thought years prior and it changed the way I look at life and business.

Before you laugh, or perhaps think I'm nuts, let me explain. Babies don't blush because they haven't yet developed a sense of self consciousness. They don't get embarrassed. If they need to pee, they pee. If they need to poop, they poop.

They're designed to try and fail, without any internal sense of judgment. If they were self-conscious, their achievement might plateau due to criticism—theirs or others. But since they're insulated from awareness, they keep exploring and growing. And think about that growth curve. In the first three years of life they go from not being able to do anything to talking, walking, speaking, and thousands of other capabilities—all because they suspended the curse of self-consciousness.

Adults? Not so much.

At some point, we become self-conscious. And in that moment, everything changes. As a general rule our tolerance for risk goes way down. We start playing safe and small.

Consider teenagers. I have three of them, so I have some thoughts on the topic. Since my teens want to fit in, naturally they don't want to stick out, like most other teenagers on the planet. They're diametrically opposed to attention. And so I've been instructed not to walk with them into school. In fact, if I see them in public, I'm not supposed to acknowledge them. They think I may embarrass them somehow. I don't worry too much because I'm told they'll grow out of it.

But let's be honest, it's not just a teenager thing. Adults don't like to feel embarrassed either. We go to great lengths to avoid looking dumb. We skip situations where we might fail. Blending in makes us comfortable. Of course, conformity looks different for adults, but for the most part we also want to wear the right things, say the right thing, and watch the right things. In a way, we're just grown up teenagers.

We sacrifice adventure in order to avoid risks. After all, risk involves the potential for failure or embarrassment. And so we sit back and watch others take risks—offering applause and admiration, but secretly we feel jealous. We know getting in the arena is an entirely different level of commitment and we're not sure we want it. Teddy Roosevelt knew this more than most and captured this dilemma his vignette referred to as "The Man in the Arena."

> It is not the critic who counts; not the man who points out how the strong man stumbles, or where the doer of deeds could have done them better. The credit belongs to the man who is actually in the arena, whose face is marred by dust and sweat and

> blood; who strives valiantly; who errs, who comes short again and again, because there is no effort without error and shortcoming; but who does actually strive to do the deeds; who knows great enthusiasms, the great devotions; who spends himself in a worthy cause; who at the best knows in the end the triumph of high achievement, and who at the worst, if he fails, at least fails while daring greatly, so that his place shall never be with those cold and timid souls who neither know victory nor defeat.[21]

The truth is we can't step into the arena without exposing ourselves to risk or embarrassment. They're intertwined. You can't have one without the other.

Embarrassment Is My ~~Middle~~ Name

I love my name—at least now. But growing up with a girl's name was a different story.

Back in the day, as a guy you didn't want a girl's name. My elementary school had several females named Carrie, Kari, and Kerry. Kids can be cruel and for some reason my name became a common focal point for some of the bullies in my class. When the guys really wanted to get under my skin they'd say hi Carrie, C-A-R-R-I-E.

THE TRUTH IS WE CAN'T STEP INTO THE ARENA WITHOUT EXPOSING OURSELVES TO RISK OR EMBARRASSMENT. THEY'RE INTERTWINED.

Looking back, I'm sure I was overly sensitive. However, since my love language is words of affirmation, back then I'd rather take a punch to the face then a sarcastic comment to the ears.

Today, I could care less about the name teasing. In fact, I invite it. When I do keynote speaking, I often start with self-deprecating humor by introducing myself as the bald guy with the girl's name. I've seen how it breaks the ice and lets the audience know that I don't take myself too seriously. As a communicator, I start by taking a risk and inviting embarrassment. The crowd often laughs and we create a memory even in the first few seconds of my talk.

This isn't just a strategy for the stage. Taking risks and inviting embarrassment is one of the traits I leverage in my entrepreneurial journey too. It's also something that helped me stay successful on my French adventure.

Every time I went to the grocery store, I could have let embarrassment stop me. I didn't know how to read the self-checkout screen or the food labels. I didn't know at which point in the process I should insert my credit card. Occasionally when it was time to pay, I pulled out my bag of coins and let the cashier make the correct change.

Restaurants were even more complex. Even with a translation app, I didn't understand the menu or the customs. I learned I shouldn't tip my server. In the first few days of the trip I declined bread at mealtimes, shocking the server and surrounding tables. Every experience brought an element of risk and embarrassment. The irony is, I didn't care because I already know it's an essential part of every new adventure. Entrepreneurship reinforces this every single day.

Back in my hometown, I know where to go, what to do, and what to say. But in the countryside of France, I wasn't sure where to fill my water bottle or how to lock the front door on my Airbnb. The property manager explained the process in French, but, of course, I didn't get it. After many minutes of back and forth app dialogue I learned I had to pull the door toward me hard and *keep holding it toward me*, while I lock and unlock the door. Failing to do the steps in this order failed to lock the door.

I had to text the poor landlord a few times, until I figured it out. The first evening, I even woke him out of bed to do so. I would have left it unlocked, but I couldn't leave my passport, laptop, and valuables unsecured. I'm sure he wondered why a grown man from America couldn't lock a door.

Climbing the First Mountain

I woke up in France on day two ready to ride. Travel delays and rain kept me inside on day one and I had a growing appetite for risk. I loaded all the routes onto my Garmin bike computer and headed out at dawn, fully stocked with snacks and electrolyte powder packs stuffed into the back of my jersey. In the first minute, I realized my routes wouldn't load right. Rather than delaying even more, I headed out in what I assumed was the correct direction.

After cycling about a mile, something didn't feel right, so I stopped and asked a townsperson which way the mountain was. She pointed 90 degrees to my right. I thanked her and then course-corrected. In the French Alps, once you get pointed in the right direction, the signs are fairly easy to follow. You just keep pedaling up and up for hours and hours on end. Some routes are more than twenty miles up, so there's no excuse for getting lost—unless you encounter a detour sign.

I found my first detour sign rather quickly. Early into my first mountain climb, I noticed a sign with a bike on it blocking the small windy road. Because I couldn't read French, I googled the image. Although I wasn't certain, I assumed I shouldn't keep traveling on this particular road, so instead, I followed the arrow. It pointed to a road that went down to the dark woods. I rode on gravel and across a wooden bridge, but eventually that detour led me back to the main road.

I loved every single moment of the challenge. True cyclists have a mutual understanding—call it an internal code of conduct. We realize cycling is pain, but we embrace it nonetheless. The suffering is kind of addicting actually. In fact, cycling greats are often quoted on this exact topic.

"Cycling is suffering."
—Fausto Coppi

"The race is won by the rider who can suffer the most."
—Eddy Merckx

Cycling is so hard, the suffering is so intense, that it's absolutely cleansing. The pain is so deep and strong

> that a curtain descends over your brain. Once; someone asked me what pleasure I took in riding for so long. "PLEASURE?" I said. "I don't understand the question. I didn't do it for the pleasure; I did it for the pain."
>
> **—Lance Armstrong**

Both risk and embarrassment include a kind of suffering because true success is never guaranteed. It's also the reason we play the game. We understand the real chance of defeat. Ask any kid if it hurts to lose. Ask any adult for that matter.

But this is why I went to France—because I wasn't sure I'd make it. I had never climbed a mountain with a bicycle before. Who knows, maybe I'd find out I couldn't do one, much less a dozen.

IT'S ALSO THE REASON WE PLAY THE GAME. WE UNDERSTAND THE REAL CHANCE OF DEFEAT.

On my first mountain alone, I thought I saw a single cyclist behind me, but I wasn't about to wait around to confirm it. I kept pedaling, stroke after stroke. By the time I reached the top of Col du Mollard, I had no water and I didn't see any restrooms. Thankfully, I spotted a helpful guy who pointed to an old school pump where I could refill my bottle. As I pumped the water, that single cyclist rode up behind me.

"Bonjour," I offered him one of the only French words I knew.

He replied with a bunch more words, but I shook my head and said, "English." Then I named the next mountain on my itinerary. "Col de Fer?"

He nodded.

Boom! I had found my first cycling buddy. We began our descent, heading to the next mountain.

Before I left Ohio, Chet texted me a number of famous mountain passes—Col de Fer being one of them. The official name, Col de la Croix de Fer, means Pass of the Iron Cross. This narrow 17-mile road nestled in the heart of the Rhône-Alpes contains a few waterfalls along the way. Other than that, it's quite isolated.

My new French friend proved to be an excellent descender. This road didn't have guardrails and he didn't seem to understand the meaning of brakes. I, on the other hand, quickly calculated the risk. I recognized if I hit a stone or missed a turn, then I'd ride off the mountain and face impending injury or death. And so, unlike my friend, I chose to engage my brakes throughout the descent. When I finally reached the bottom of the mountain, I spotted him a long way off, but at least I knew I was headed in the right direction. On various switchbacks, I'd see him ahead of me, but then, I'd turn and he faded from my sight.

Originally, I had planned to listen to multiple audio books while I rode. I thought I'd get bored. After all, these rides in the Alps certainly surpassed my previous record of five hours on a bicycle. But the breathtaking views removed any need for audiobooks. Besides, it might disrupt my concentration, and I felt my life was more valuable than consuming content. So, I stayed engaged and aware of my surroundings.

The mind goes many places when you ride alone surrounded by beauty. I prayed. I dreamed. And I thought about my new role as the chair of the entrepreneurship program at the university.

As I progressed up the mountain, the winding roads revealed many names that super fans spray painted on the road the year before. Newer to the sport of cycling, I still recognized one in particular—Jonas Vingegaard, the eventual winner of the Tour de France. Col de Fer served as stage 12 on the Tour de France the year before. I smiled, realizing I was climbing the same mountain as the best cyclists in the world. Of course, they had conquered the Alps much faster than me, but this truth helped me tap into a new mental level.

Even Bigger Than the Mountain

As narrow as these roads were, I was shocked to see a car descending the mountain heading right for me. I quickly found out this is a thing in France. Sports cars and motorcycles often summit the mountains after the majority of the snow melts.

When the cars came at me, forcing me closer to the edge of the cliff—the cliff with no guardrails—I stayed focused by staring at the small section of the road in front of me. Despite the nervous energy vibrating throughout my body I kept on advancing higher and higher. When cars weren't threatening my life, I kept an eye out for the road signs posted every kilometer. These signs became my friends. Each one counted down how much further I had to go before I reached the top and what percentage of incline I could expect throughout the next kilometer.

One thing you want to pay attention to when climbing mountains is your gear ratio. This is the number of times the rear wheel turns for each full turn of the pedals. It's calculated by dividing the number of teeth on the chain ring by the number of teeth on the rear cog. Before I left the United States, I made sure my gear ratio was optimized for cycling in the mountains.

Cyclists call their lowest gear their granny gear. It's the smallest chain ring on a crank. I stayed in mine for most of the ride up the mountain. Finally, as I neared the top, I saw the Frenchman ahead of me. Although he crushed me on the decline, I took the incline a bit faster than him. As I reached my riding companion, I said "Bonjour!" Then I repeated, "Oui! Oui! Oui!" In English I intended to tell him, "Hello. Yes! Yes! Yes!"

That's pretty much all the French I knew. I said his name a few times and gave him some fist pumps before I passed him. He returned the smile back at me. We kept on ascending the mountain in the scorching summer heat.

When we finally got to the top, I wasn't sure what to do. I saw another group of cyclists that must have climbed the back side of the mountain. They huddled around a sign taking pictures. The sign said:

Col de la Croix de Fer Altitude 2067 m

My French friend and I traded phones and took a couple of pictures. I sent the images to my friends back home in our group text. Some replied with encouragement. Others said they wished they could be there.

I felt a deep sense of joy. Halfway around the world, on top of a beautiful mountain, I was connected to God, myself, and even my friends.

Some may think it's foolish to risk so much and climb all that way just to take a picture. But for me, it wasn't about the external picture—not even close. Rather, it was about the internal challenge I had overcome. Anytime we do hard things, as athletes or entrepreneurs, we strengthen our confidence and competence. Achievement is like a muscle. Develop it in one area and you can't help but benefit from it in other areas too.

Repeating Risk Regularly

At the top of Col de Fer, I couldn't find a place to refill my water bottles.

Dehydration is a real threat and so I walked toward a few motorcycles. I found someone who spoke both French and English and asked him if he knew where I could find water. He opened his bag, pulled out a large container of water, and graciously refilled my bottles. I thanked him profusely and asked if he could also interpret for me and my new French cyclist friend.

ACHIEVEMENT IS LIKE A MUSCLE. DEVELOP IT IN ONE AREA AND YOU CAN'T HELP BUT BENEFIT FROM IT IN OTHER AREAS TOO.

Through my interpreter, I asked my riding companion where he was going next. He said he would be heading through Glandon and then back to his hometown. I told him I had planned to go further all the way to Alpe d'Huez. He shook his head and said no way—or the French equivalent. He said after doing Col de Fer it would be a mistake to try to continue. Instead, he recommended I follow him back. Even though I really thought I could do the rest of the route, I figured he knew best.

We strapped on our helmets and headed down the backside of the mountain—the Frenchman faster than me. But by now, I started to feel a *little* more comfortable (emphasis on the word little). We descended to Glandon, and then all the way to the small towns below. When we reached his village, he pointed down the road several times. I assumed this meant goodbye forever and I kept pedaling to St. Jean de Maurienne.

After cycling another seven miles, I arrived back at the Airbnb around 1 PM and spent a few minutes struggling to open the door. Inviting embarrassment yet again, I texted the landlord for his assistance. He kindly showed me how to solve the door dilemma and I thanked him. This task was also becoming a *little* more comfortable too.

Despite my body feeling tired, my mind felt more alive than ever. I sat down at the table and prepared a meal of more smoked salmon, avocado, dates, cheese, and water.

I had an interesting thought. Since it was only two in the afternoon, "What if I took a risk and climbed another mountain before sunset?"

I texted Chet and told him how amazing my day had been. He called back right away and asked what I planned to do next. I told him I wanted to climb the lacets to Col de la Madeleine. From the moment I first saw a picture of Les Lacets de Montvernier—the French phrase for "'The Shoelaces of Montvernier"—I couldn't get it out of my mind. This route "scales the cliff face above the Maurienne valley, as if a shoelace had been dropped from the sky."[22]

This ride ranks as number two on the "Top Ten Craziest Switchback Cycle Climbs in the World" by the website *Gran Fondo*, an Italian term which loosely translates to "Big Ride." According to the article, "The Lacets are only about 20% of the climb to Chaussy, with 17 hairpins stacked one on top of another in just 3 km, an astonishing piece of mountain road engineering."

(Click the link or scan the QR code to enjoy the Lacelets.)

Reader's Digest ranked it #2 in their article titled, *18 of the Most Dangerous Roads in the World*.[23] True to French construction, this route contained little to no true guardrails, and believe it or not, bikes share all those curves with cars. If you encounter a car, then you have very little space, and once again, you risk falling off the mountain. As scary as it was, I enjoyed the adrenaline I experienced on these climbs.

Risk Bearers

Some people incorrectly think entrepreneurship is for adrenaline junkies addicted to risk-taking. However, E-Minds emphasize *cal-*

culated risk taking. Of course, some people just enjoy epinephrine, the neurotransmitter and hormone, also known as adrenaline. However, for entrepreneurs there's a deeper purpose at stake.

Entrepreneurs understand adrenaline isn't the end goal, but rather a means to the goal.

Pure adrenaline junkies seek roller coasters and death-defying experiences to feel a rush, not to create value for clients and customers. Entrepreneurs seek a higher purpose, innovating to benefit others. After all, this is the only way they're financially compensated. Entrepreneurship and risk go hand-in-hand. A quick look at the etymology proves this. The word literally means "bearer of risk." It's a French word, "coined by Jean-Baptiste Say from the word entreprendre—usually translated as 'undertaker' or 'adventurer.'"[24]

ENTREPRENEURS UNDERSTAND ADRENALINE ISN'T THE END GOAL, BUT RATHER A MEANS TO THE GOAL.

According to Investopedia, "An entrepreneur is an individual who creates a new business, bearing most of the risks and enjoying most of the rewards. They're commonly seen as an innovator, a source of new ideas, goods, services, and business/or procedures. "[25]

Simply put, entrepreneurs are *comfortable* with being *uncomfortable* and comfortable with other people rejecting them and their ideas. In my book, *The Deeper Path*, I shared how people dismissed entrepreneurs. Here are a few examples of *people* getting rejected[26]:

- They rejected Christopher Columbus.
  So many centuries after the Creation it is unlikely that anyone could find hitherto unknown lands of any value.
  —Committee advising King Ferdinand and Queen Isabella of Spain regarding a proposal by Christopher Columbus, 1486

- They rejected Babe Ruth.
  Taking the best left-handed pitcher in baseball and converting him into a right fielder is one of the dumbest things I ever heard.
  —Tris Speaker, baseball expert, talking about Babe Ruth, 1919

- They rejected The Beatles.
  We don't like their sound, and guitar music is on the way out.
  —Decca Records, when they rejected The Beatles, 1962

- They rejected Apple® Co-founders.
  So then we went to, and they said, "Hey, we don't need you. You haven't got through college yet."
  —Steve Jobs, founder of Apple Computer, Inc., on his and Steve Wozniak's early attempts to distribute their personal computer.

Other times, entrepreneurs were dismissed for their ideas. Here are few examples of *products* getting rejected:

- They rejected personal computers.
  There is no reason anyone would want a computer in their home.
  —Ken Olson, president, chairman, and founder of Digital Equipment Corp. (DEC), maker of big business mainframe computers, arguing against the PC, 1977

- They rejected the radio.
  The wireless music box has no imaginable commercial value. Who would pay for a message sent to no one in particular?
  —Associates of David Sarnoff responding to the latter's call for investment in the radio, 1921

- They rejected automobiles.
  The horse is here to stay but the automobile is only a novelty—a fad.
  —The president of the Michigan Savings Bank advising Henry Ford's lawyer, Horace Rackham, not to invest in the Ford Motor Co., 1903

- They rejected the telephone.
  This "telephone" has too many shortcomings to be seriously considered as a means of communication. The device is inherently of no value to us.
  —A memo at Western Union, 1878

Last time I checked, nobody loves rejection, whether it's directed at themselves or their ideas. So how do we transcend this very real emotional response? Although it's simple, it's not always easy.

The trick is making friends with risk and embarrassment—the Third Trait of the E-Mind.

Sometimes embarrassment results from the idea itself. Perhaps it's too innovative or too disruptive. Other times embarrassment results from the timing of the launch. Perhaps it's too early or too unproven.

Reed Hoffman, the co-founder of LinkedIn®, says, "If you're not embarrassed by the first version of your product, you've launched too late."[27] Entrepreneurial thinkers understand embarrassment is an ally and a teacher by showing us what we've missed or what we've done wrong. It's much easier to avoid embarrassment. This is why some people never launch. But there's a problem with that strategy. These same people never get feedback either. Launching is scary and it requires risk.

I teach all my entrepreneurs: *Market before you manufacture.* I dedicated an entire chapter to the idea in my book *Day Job to Dream Job*. When you market before you manufacture, you intentionally launch before you're ready. This allows you to gather data, and perhaps early funding, even before an official product release.

Look no further than GoFundMe® or Kickstarter. These platforms encourage MVPs.

A minimum viable product (MVP) is a concept coined by Frank Robinson and popularized in the *Lean Startup* methodology and respective book written by Eric Ries. An MVP is a basic version of a product that's as simple as possible, with only the core features that meet the target audience's needs. The goal of an MVP is to create and test new products or services allowing a team to learn as much as possible about customers with the least amount of effort.

Rather than theorizing in a sanitized environment with fabricated conditions, going to market produces real world data in real time. Movie trailers are one such example. Releasing a trailer prior to a launch elicits customer feedback. Social media platforms are never shy about opinions. This scares some creators and encourages others.

Bestselling author and marketing guru Seth Godin understands the need to launch before we're ready. He says:

> The only purpose of starting is to finish, and while the projects we do are never really finished, they must ship. Perfect doesn't mean flawless. Perfect means it does exactly what I need it to do. A vacation can be perfect even if the nuts on the plane weren't warmed before serving. Any project that's held up in revisions and meetings and general fear-based polishing is the victim of a crime. It's a crime because you're stealing that perfect work from a customer who will benefit from it. You're holding back the good stuff from the people who need it, afraid of what the people who don't will say. Stop polishing and ship instead. Polished perfect isn't better than perfect, it's merely shinier. And late.[28]

I encourage entrepreneurs to view their future customers as travelers wandering in the desert, in desperate need of their water. Could they take longer polishing the glass before serving them the water? Sure. Do people care? Not that much.

If you're holding up a launch because you're afraid of looking foolish, then you're actually harming your future client.

You're prideful, because you're focused more on yourself than helping others. We may try to justify our motives for delaying, but the truth is we care more about our reputation than creating value in the marketplace.

IF YOU'RE HOLDING UP A LAUNCH BECAUSE YOU'RE AFRAID OF LOOKING FOOLISH, THEN YOU'RE ACTUALLY HARMING YOUR FUTURE CLIENT.

Failing to Finish

On day two, I kept climbing Les Lacets de Montvernier on my way to Col du Chaussy. I felt great because I had slept well the night before. Each small village I passed looked like a fairytale. Actually, the word village is too big. These regions were simply a collection of houses with a church and a water fountain. That's it. No food or restrooms, just a church and water. I loved it, and since I wasn't in a rush, I soaked up every moment of beauty.

I climbed all the way to the top of the mountain. The whole time, I saw only one other cyclist. I almost felt guilty savoring these otherworldly landscapes all by myself. I pedaled to the lone structure on top of the mountain, a restaurant called Auberge du Chaussy. Two older couples sat outside at a table drinking coffee and chatting. They stared at me and so I used my default greeting, "Bonjour."

"Bonjour," they reciprocated

Nearly out of water again, I went inside and tried to order some food. Though they were technically closed, the server let me order coffee and dessert. One item looked especially good, and it had what looked like the word lemon in the name. But whatever that word was, it wasn't lemon. It turned out to be a muffin—the first muffin I had eaten in about fifteen years.

After all this climbing, I didn't care about carbs.

The waitress then brought out the smallest coffee I'd ever seen. It was no bigger than a thimble. The locals a few tables over kept laughing—probably at me. I smiled, surmising I had probably done yet another culturally incorrect offense. I invited the embarrassment and simply waved back at them. I was having the time of my life, the perfect adventure. I would never see these people again, nor did I need to impress them. All these new experiences offered education and embarrassment.

After my dessert and coffee, I decided to skip Col de la Madeleine and head back to my Airbnb. The sun was sinking and I didn't want to take unnecessary risks and stay on the mountain longer than I should. I didn't pack lights or cold weather gear and I'd already enjoyed a perfect day. This is wisdom—something I haven't always embodied. It's the difference between taking foolish risks and calculated risks—a wise entrepreneur knows the difference.

It reminds me of one of my favorites stories:

> Suppose one of you wants to build a tower. Won't you first sit down and estimate the cost to see if you

> have enough money to complete it? For if you lay the foundation and are not able to finish it, everyone who sees it will ridicule you, saying, "This person began to build and wasn't able to finish." Or suppose a king is about to go to war against another king. Won't he first sit down and consider whether he is able with ten thousand men to oppose the one coming against him with twenty thousand? If he is not able, he will send a delegation while the other is still a long way off and will ask for terms of peace.[29]

Embarrassment Is My Ally

So many times during my France adventure, I invited embarrassment. Growth and progress require it. One morning after clocking many miles, I descended into Italy. I wanted to cross the border since I'd never been there. After a quick pic, I headed back into France, facing a significant climb.

Low on energy, I knew I needed some calories. I vowed to stop at whatever restaurant I saw next. After a few miles, I spotted an older building that might serve food. I got off my bicycle and walked into the bar. The entire menu was in French. Although they were closed too, the waitress mentioned some kind of salami thing they served. I'm really not a fan of salami, especially when cycling. I asked if I could order a simple salad with lettuce, cheese, and tomato instead. She nodded.

While I waited, I asked for a fork. She looked at me like I was crazy. I assumed the word fork didn't translate well, so I explained what a fork looked like. She shook her head in disbelief, but she brought me one nonetheless. Then a few minutes later she brought out a plate with my "salad."

When I looked at the plate I broke out laughing and then she joined in laughing too. Rather than a salad, she brought me the biggest lettuce, cheese, and tomato sandwich I'd ever seen. The fresh baked bread looked incredible, even for a guy who doesn't eat bread. Now I knew why she thought I was crazy. A fork wasn't going to be much help.

I realized on that mountain in order to come out on top—literally and figuratively—I'd have to get used to taking risks—big ones and small ones. Inviting embarrassment would be necessary if I wanted to eat, drink, and learn how to lock my rental apartment. On that mountain, I also realized this little trip to France might be bigger than cycling. In the beginning, I thought it was just about my trip.

But then I started to see how this trip was a microcosm for how to think like an entrepreneur. I started to see the Ten Traits in action and then I started thinking about you, my future reader. Maybe your life is much bigger than you could imagine. Maybe you're supposed to learn how to think like an entrepreneur because God has an important assignment for you. Maybe you're supposed to change someone's world and you need to learn how to tap into the E-Mind.

Maybe you need to master:

1. **Independence**: No One Is Coming To Save You

2. **Flexibility**: Map It Out, Then Make It Up

3. **Risk**: Embarrassment Is Your Ally

And maybe you need to discover the other seven traits so you can enjoy an exponential advantage.

After I finished the best sandwich of my life—without a fork, mind you—I decided right then I was going to turn this trip into a book to help others learn and leverage the E-Mind. Then I got back on my bicycle and kept on climbing one pedal stroke at a time.

Whether you think you can or you think you can't, you're right.

—Henry Ford

Trait Four: Teachability

Learn the Language and Culture

"What's in the box?" the gentleman asked me in a French accent.

I sat on a bench, eating a Chia bar waiting for the bus on my first day. I explained it was my bicycle and that I would be cycling the French Alps.

His eyes lit up and he and his wife made small talk with me, sharing their backpack trip through Europe. This man, a couple of decades older than me, showed pictures from his phone about his other passion, scaling ice formations with a pick ax. I was impressed by his appetite for adventure. After we chatted for a bit, I pulled out a Chia protein bar and offered him one. He resisted at first, but finally accepted.

In return, he gave me an unopened, small cardboard carton. I gladly accepted, though I couldn't read the French label. I thought it best to ask him the contents before I drink it. After a bit of translating, together we figured out it was almond milk.

"See, it's rated B. This means it is *very* good for you," he said pointing to a chart on the carton. "In France they rate food and drinks for us."

The man taught me something. With my curiosity piqued, I discovered more about this cultural mandate with a quick search on my smartphone. Evidently, the Nutri-Score, also known as the 5 Color Nutrition label, is a rating system, and an attempt to simplify the overall nutritional value of food products. It assigns products a rating letter from A (best) to E (worst), with associated colors from green to red.

Later that night at the grocery store, I stayed teachable and I took that knowledge to heart. His explanation of the language and culture helped me navigate the experience and make better decisions, faster. Thanks to him, I didn't ignorantly load up my shopping cart with "E" categorized food and drink. If I had, I might have bonked on the mountain when nutrition mattered most.

It's not About You

As I've taught my business clients for nearly two decades, if we're not careful, we end up focusing too much on ourselves. We observe this in big and small ways. For example, too often we create products or services that solve *our* problems. We choose packaging based on *our* preferences. We settle on a logo and color that makes sense to *us*.

Without any malicious intent, we can inadvertently make ourselves the center of our businesses. Then we wonder why sales are slow and profits are low.

WITHOUT ANY MALICIOUS INTENT, WE CAN INADVERTENTLY MAKE OURSELVES THE CENTER OF OUR BUSINESSES. THEN WE WONDER WHY SALES ARE SLOW AND PROFITS ARE LOW.

In his book, *Building a StoryBrand*, bestselling author Donald Miller's main premise is that customers want to hire a guide, not a hero. Instead, customers want to be the hero—like "Luke Skywalker" or "Neo"—and find a guide—like "Yoda" or "Morpheus." Unfortunately, most businesses, institutions, and brands, make themselves the hero. Rather than staying teachable to their clients, they slip into a "me" focused frenzy, acting like they possess all the knowledge and answers.

When we fail to learn our customer's language and culture, we "miss" them—not to mention their needs and desires. We arrogantly assume we know what's best. This classic mistake costs brands big money and time. E-Minds are different. By thinking like entrepreneurs we start with teachability. We learn the language and the culture and then we internalize that knowledge. This clarity shapes the way we do everything else: creation all the way to communication. The result is simple and undeniable. It leads to conversions—and many of them. I call this process *The Teachability Track™*.

Culture => Creation => Communication => Conversion

Here's a breakdown of the four steps. We begin by taking time to learn the culture. This requires humility. It means we admit we don't know everything. Instead we come ready to listen and learn. Once we understand clients and their needs, only then do we move into creation mode. We integrate their preferred features into our design, ensuring our design offers the true benefits they need. Then we communicate this customer awareness within our sales and marketing process. This creates an empathy bridge that strengthens the relationship. By demonstrating expertise, through the Teachability Track, we experience more customer conversions, that is, people who buy our products and services.

Leveraging the Language

As you know by now, when I arrived overseas, my knowledge of French was non-existent. Still, I knew to be successful in France I'd better learn how to communicate. Early in the trip, I discovered new tools like Google Translate. By holding my smart phone over French menus, I benefited from augmented reality technology. I could then "read" the menu and order with confidence.

I also leveraged a few key phrases, and by a few, I mean three: *bonjour*, *merci*, and *oui*. But I blended these phrases with a teachable tone and a commitment to embody the second Trait of the E-Mind: Risk. My limited knowledge of French pushed me to use hand signs and body language. When I passed cyclists, I nodded to greet them. I figured out how to give rough signs for water and money. Smiling and waving went a long way in communicating friendliness. Fortunately, those universal gestures communicate across many different people groups. By making embarrassment my ally, the kind French people sensed my heart and overlooked much of my ignorance. We got along beautifully.

I also made a point to learn French culture, every opportunity I had, even regarding their view about air conditioning. Evidently, in France it's not as popular as back in the United States—even on hot summer days. A deeper dive revealed that many French people have a stigma regarding air conditioning. There's a real conversation about how it makes people sick and more susceptible to getting sore throats and even catching colds. At first, I didn't know if the French believed this, but then I found a mountain of content on the topic like this blog post titled: *Why are the French afraid of air conditioning*?[30] Another blogger named Nasse posted an article titled: *Why is there never any air conditioning in France?*[31] In the article, she gives multiple reasons for this cultural belief.

As an outsider, I could have had several potential responses to a view different from my own. I could have:

1. Debated them.
2. Changed them—or tried to.
3. Stayed teachable.

I chose the third option and I'm glad I did. I would have wasted a ton of time and energy trying to change a country to fit my view.

Entrepreneurs encounter these differences regularly. They can fight cultures within organizations or they can adapt and evolve by staying teachable.

In France, these cultural differences popped up in the most unexpected ways. I learned how certain public transportation required special train tickets. I learned that I couldn't bring a backpack into certain bathrooms at certain tourist locations. I learned that restaurants don't fill water bottles for cyclists, but if I ordered a bottle of sparkling water first, then they'd refill my water bottles. I learned that a cup of coffee is actually a tiny cup of espresso.

I also learned the French run according to a different view of time. One day, I was experiencing gear trouble on my bicycle toward the end of a ride. So the next morning, I woke up early and went to the cycling store. I figured since it was a Monday morning, they'd be open and without many other customers. When I arrived at the store, the gentleman opened his locked door and told me to come back at two in the afternoon. He told me the store would be open four hours and then close back up at six o'clock.

I had a choice. Would I stay teachable and adjust or would I dig my heels in and tell him he was wrong? Stubbornness wouldn't have done much good. Instead of riding that day, I decided to make it a rest day. I used the morning to catch up on work via my laptop back at the room.

I returned that afternoon fifteen minutes early. A line quickly formed behind me. The kind gentleman took a few minutes to fix the derailleur, and he charged a small fee to fix it. The following day, I wanted to achieve a big goal—climbing 15,000 feet of elevation. It was the hardest day I'd ever done—eleven hours on a bike—so repairing those gears was critical. I'm so glad I stayed teachable and adjusted to their schedule.

Adapting to the Culture

When we encounter new cultures in work or life, we have a choice. We can make the world adapt to us or we can adapt to culture.

No matter how much I tried, I wasn't going to transition the country from measuring in meters to miles. And so as I made my way through France, I quickly made the mental switch. I converted the 2,500-meter elevation signs to 7,500 feet. I readjusted my expectations and my oxygen levels. I also stayed teachable regarding the temperature, converting Celcius to Fahrenheit, and packing appropriate sunscreen.

WHEN WE ENCOUNTER NEW CULTURES IN WORK OR LIFE, WE HAVE A CHOICE. WE CAN MAKE THE WORLD ADAPT TO US OR WE CAN ADAPT TO CULTURE.

Entrepreneurs encounter many different kinds of languages and customs while creating their businesses. At times we need to study new terms for new industries. Perhaps we need to brush up on verbiage related to different customer avatars and their demographic and psychographics nuances.

When I left the church world and entered the business world, I had to remain teachable and learn a new language and culture. This doesn't mean I forgot my identity or that I became a culture chameleon. Rather, I embraced the role of the learner and adapted my approach to connect with my clients and customers on non essentials. As I created value, I earned rapport, and this rapport provided a platform for other people to see and hear my message.

The Apostle Paul, an entrepreneur at heart, embodied this strategy. He told his followers:

To the Jews I became like a Jew, to win the Jews. To those under the law I became like one under the law (though I myself am not under the law), so as to win those under the law. To those not having the law I became like one not having the law (though I am not free from God's law but am under Christ's law), so as to win those not having the law. To the weak I became weak, to win the weak. I have become all things to all people so that by all possible means I might save some.[32]

Paul stayed teachable and as a result, many people converted. He changed his medium, but kept his message consistent.

Even most recently, with my new role at the university, I've needed to learn and relearn some of the nuances surrounding higher education. I've explored the difference between assistant professor, associate professor, and full professor. I can now better distinguish between half-time, three-quarter-time, and full-time. I've familiarized myself with topics of tenure, curriculum, and accreditation. And as we'll unpack in the near future with another Trait, I had to make friends before I needed them.

Every industry has their own language and culture. If we want to succeed in new places with new people, then we must remain teachable. People sense our authenticity by our body language. They want to work with someone who is real and understands their concerns, needs, and language. This means we foster a mindset of teachability. When we see every person as someone we can learn from, we increase our vocabulary, and each encounter expands our potential to succeed.

Teachability Requires Humility

Learning from every person we meet requires humility. Pride deceives us into thinking we know everything. And when we develop that kind of mindset, we become unteachable. These types of people fall far short of their potential.

> PRIDE DECEIVES US INTO THINKING WE KNOW EVERYTHING. AND WHEN WE DEVELOP THAT KIND OF MINDSET, WE BECOME UNTEACHABLE.

Learning the culture of France required humility on more than one occasion. At the top of Col du Galibier, I found myself without water—again. I had just ascended a very hard 8,668 foot mountain. After all that climbing, I was hungry too. It was almost noon, so I found the closest restaurant. Actually, it was the only restaurant. A man and woman greeted me from one of the tables outside. Thanks to Google Translate, they told me they would be happy to serve me soon. They're exact words were, "We're eating right now. We can help you in ten minutes."

In American culture, I would have been the priority. At least one of them would have stopped eating to take my order. But I had entered their world, so I had to adjust my schedule into French time. It didn't matter that I was running late or that I had much more cycling to pack in that day. The casual atmosphere of the country didn't account for me having a tight time schedule. They were not being rude, just French, a culture that seldom rushes.

As entrepreneurs, we have to meet our clients where they are, recognize the subtle cultural differences, and walk in humility as we learn to adapt.

In France, I learned to humble myself when I wanted to eat in a hurry. I either ordered something pre-made or at a sit-down restaurant I ordered the appetizer, main dish, and dessert all at once and then I handed the server my credit card. The waitstaff sometimes looked at me kind of funny, but when I needed to pack in a lot of cycling, I didn't have an hour and a half to eat lunch on French time.

I learned the language and then I leveraged the language.

Teachability Means It's Not about You

Phil Knight, co-founder of Nike and author of the memoir *Shoe Dog*, shares in his book how he studied the culture of the countries he entered. Steve Jobs obsessively analyzed competitors and their products. It's much easier to transform an industry after you first learn the industry.

Of course, this Trait requires wisdom and balance. Teachability doesn't mean you simply surrender your core values or abandon your mission. Elon Musk was highly criticized for rejecting Twitter culture back in 2022 when he took the company private. Just based on the numbers alone, something had to change. Time will be the ultimate judge; however, no one can argue he initiated radical transformation.

This fourth Trait is both an art and a science. Just because you're teachable doesn't mean your customer is always right. Many companies identify their employees as their first customers, not the patrons who frequent their facilities. Wise entrepreneurs have zero tolerance for customers who abuse their team members.

I successfully navigated France on a solo mission because I committed to stay teachable. I took imperfect action and kept studying the culture. Although I made a ton of mistakes, I embodied humility along the way. In the process, I had a ton of fun too.

Entrepreneurs travel the same path, learning the language and then leveraging the language. But this isn't where we end.

We're just getting started.

Knowledge is as infinite as the universe.

The man who claims to know all, only reveals to all that he really knows nothing.

—Suzy Kassem

Trait Five: Resourcefulness

LEVERAGE THE CORRECT CURRENCY

"Three euro please," the French woman said to me.

"Do you take Visa?" I asked.

"Oui, but if you use your Visa, there's an extra charge of five euro," she replied empathetically.

On my second day of cycling, I took the train to Modane, a border town of Italy. I knew I'd face some incredibly difficult mountains that day. The plan was to climb Mont Cenis, and then descend into Italy. From there, I'd head back to France and climb Col de I'Iseran. I thought I'd better get some breakfast before confronting those desolate mountains.

I exited the train station and scanned the street, spotting a bakery. I thought they might have some breakfast foods. I had already surrendered any attempts at Keto in France. Once inside, I picked out a chocolate croissant and coffee. The kind young lady behind the counter spoke a little English. She prepared the order and shared the price. When I told her I didn't have any euros, she explained the Visa upcharge.

"Is there a currency exchange around?" I asked. I wasn't thrilled about paying an extra fee of nearly twice the price of my breakfast just to use my Visa.

She understood my dilemma and pointed down the road. "ATM."

I said I'd return with her preferred currency, knowing I should have prepared better.

Correct Currency Matters

At the end of the Civil War, the Confederate currency lost its value nearly overnight. Many wealthy southerners said goodbye to fortunes realizing that not all paper is equal.

That wasn't the first time currencies shifted. In ancient times, people were paid in salt. This truth inspired the phrase, "She's not worth her salt." It also influenced words like salary. Today, we'd laugh at employers who pay with salt.

Throughout history, eggs, grain, and other commodities were just as valuable as the money we use today: like gold, silver, stocks, bitcoin, and credit cards. While many think in terms of dollars, pesos, euros, and yuan, the true definition of currency is an acceptable "medium of exchange."[33]

Entrepreneurs understand the importance of resourcefulness and leveraging the correct currency. They know currency transcends dollars and cents. Successful E-Minds must earn many types of currency: social, relational, educational, and trust to name a few.

The Chinese proverb exhorts us to, "Dig a well before you need it." Wise entrepreneurs aim for abundance, not debt. They store up a surplus of currency.

I should have been better prepared in Modane. If so, the process would have been much smoother. In fact, I should have found a currency exchange earlier in my trip. Unfortunately, I had a lapse and failed to be resourceful.

The dictionary defines resourcefulness as the ability to find quick and clever ways to overcome difficulties.[34] In my book, *Show Up, Filled Up*, I encourage entrepreneurs to approach every relationship as a giver, ready to deliver value. This means being resourceful and doing the work before meeting with investors. Anticipate their questions. Develop responses for potential objections. If you know potential clients may be at the same event, research their recent history. Look at their posts. Listen to their podcasts. Watch their videos. Surprise them by knowing their updates before they even share them. This shows you care and that you're interested in their future success, not just a future sale.

Never tell people you respect, "Hey, if you ever need anything, just reach out. I'm here for you." This type of response screams unawareness. Although well-intended, your job is to know what they need before they even know it. By doing so, you earn credibility.

I ENCOURAGE ENTREPRENEURS TO APPROACH EVERY RELATIONSHIP AS A GIVER, READY TO DELIVER VALUE.

Credibility Increases Your Currency

In 1992, George H.W. Bush and Bill Clinton participated in a town hall debate.[35] A woman in the crowd asked President Bush about issues surrounding inflation, the economy, and national debt. She wanted to know how he could personally relate to those issues since he came from wealth and served in Washington, DC.

Rather than remaining present, President Bush checked his watch. He then went on to try and answer the question. Although he didn't really understand the question, he explained what it's like to live in the White House and get letters addressed to the President. He lost credibility by standing far away from her—literally. Rather than serving, he tried making her understand how *he* felt with the pressures that come with leading the most powerful country in the world.

Bill Clinton did the opposite. Rather than giving facts and figures, he used relational currency. Clinton stepped toward the woman. He asked clarifying questions. Then he shared how people in his state were deeply affected by the pain brought on by the strained economy. He shared how he personally knew the people who had suffered financial loss.

Many historians identify this exchange as a pivotal moment in the debate and the Presidential Campaign of 1992. Some even go so far as to say it was the event that led to Bill Clinton winning the presidency and preventing George H. W. Bush from serving a second term.

No one can argue how Bill Clinton gained credibility from this town hall debate. What made it so pronounced was the contrast between him and Bush. Clinton emerged as a man of the people. Bush, on the other hand, exited as an out-of-touch politician.

By embodying resourcefulness, Clinton gained credibility. He leveraged that momentum to gain even more currency which carried him successfully all the way to the White House.

The Currency Cycle

Relational currency goes a long way. President Theodore Roosevelt knew this and eloquently said, "No one cares how much you know until they know how much you care."

When people sense someone truly cares, they reciprocate with trust. This trust keeps piling up as a form of currency. What do you do with that stockpile of goodwill?

Any entrepreneur will tell you there's a time to lead stakeholders through a period of uncertainty. This means "spending" some of that goodwill. Perhaps it's during a rebrand or new product launch. Regardless, when entrepreneurs lead through uncharted waters they often need to "cash in" some of the currency they've amassed over time.

Steve Jobs was famous for this. When he launched a new Apple product, thousands of people stood in line—literally. They voted with their wallets simply because he had built so much relational equity. By staying resourceful and delivering on past promises, Steve Jobs kept innovating betting that super fans would show their support.

Elon Musk regularly taps into this Trait too. It's why SpaceX® secured contracts from NASA early on, and it's why NASA keeps coming back for more. It's also why he attracts a loyal group of highly talented teammates that follow him to whatever new company he launches or acquires. Of course not everyone likes him. But no one can deny his knack for earning credibility.

> BY STAYING RESOURCEFUL AND DELIVERING ON PAST PROMISES, STEVE JOBS KEPT INNOVATING BETTING THAT SUPER FANS WOULD SHOW THEIR SUPPORT.

This Trait transcends the rocket industry. Many shoe manufacturers have a long-standing history of quality and workmanship. Some have become so popular it's dangerous to wear them in certain areas of the United States. TOMS® shoes didn't start out this way. Hardly any new product does. TOMS shoes founder Blake Mycoskie came on the scene in 2006. His shoes went from unknown to available in five hundred retailers in just six years. Credibility took TOMS to the top.

It's obvious to see why. After Mycoskie visited Argentina, he wanted to help kids who didn't have shoes. As a result he leveraged his resources—an online drivers' education company and a passion to help kids in South America. He dreamt up a "buy one, give one" business model. People didn't purchase his shoes because of the quality. Rather, they bought into his vision: to put shoes on the feet of children in need. He earned social currency—and his vision to help children in need gave him enormous credibility.

Mycoskie enjoyed the benefits of the Currency Cycle™.

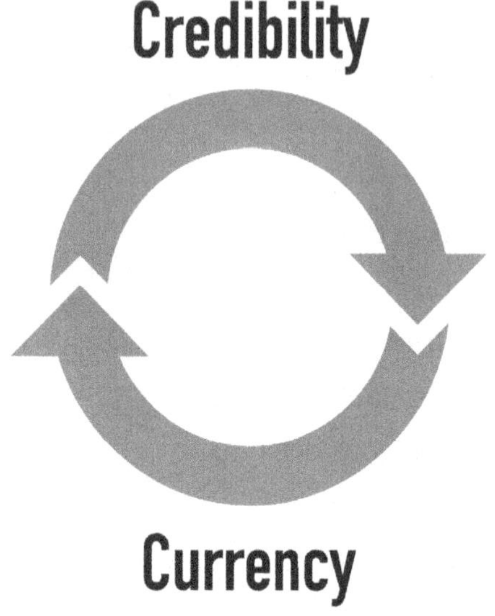

The top arrow represents credibility and the bottom one represents currency. The two arrows move around the circle. As you gain more credibility, your currency increases. As your currency increases, your credibility increases. By leveraging this concept, you'll enjoy ever-increasing value creation.

Turning Your Resources into Currency

E-Minds are constantly looking for new ways to increase currency. Resourcefulness doesn't mean you have a ton of wealth. It means you have the eyes to see what's around you and turn it into currency. Look no further than the television show *MacGyver.* The lead character was famous for embodying resourcefulness. All he needed was duct tape and paper clips—or some other household item. He leveraged these materials to detonate bombs and rescue hostages.

Resourceful people never focus on what they don't have. They only see possibilities, and they transform these possibilities into currency—something they can use as a medium for exchange.

Recently *America's Got Talent* welcomed a comedian who faces insurmountable challenges everyday. Ahren Belisle has cerebral palsy. He can't speak. His left arm is shriveled. And his left leg doesn't move well. His service dog Al joins him on stage when he performs. Every judge wondered how someone with these kinds of disabilities could be a stand-up comic.

RESOURCEFUL PEOPLE NEVER FOCUS ON WHAT THEY DON'T HAVE. THEY ONLY SEE POSSIBILITIES, AND THEY TRANSFORM THESE POSSIBILITIES INTO CURRENCY—SOMETHING THEY CAN USE AS A MEDIUM FOR EXCHANGE.

But Ahren has currencies the judges didn't know about—intellectual currency and emotional currency for starters. He knows how to leverage these currencies too. This young entrepreneur mastered other E-Mind Traits, like Risk. Throughout his career, he's made embarrassment his ally. This fuels his success.

He wears a contagious smile that captivates audiences and he communicates by a realistic text-to-speech to deliver his lines. His comedic currency incites laughter, giving him enough time to type his next funny quip. He quickly became a crowd favorite and their support propelled him into the next round.

Ahren's story might be unique, but many entrepreneur's stories contain common elements of struggle and hardship. Dolly

Parton experienced this firsthand. She's known across music genres, and her Imagination Library provides books to young children around the world. But the country music legend has very humble beginnings. This daughter of an illiterate tobacco farmer grew up in poverty. Going to Nashville equipped with the only resources she had—the currencies of talent and a personality bigger than her five-foot-tall frame—she struggled her way to the top of her industry.

The result? According to Parade.com, "Dolly Parton has a net worth of...$650 million. It has been speculated that the singer could have achieved billionaire status if she were not so generous with her money, constantly investing in many philanthropic end eavors."[36] For sixty years, Dolly Parton has made resourcefulness a daily habit.

Resourcefulness Can Silence the Stakeholders

One female entrepreneur who secured billionaire status is Sara Blakely. She created what is a global product now, but in the beginning no one wanted what she sold. Research revealed that males owned every other women's hosiery company, so she started using a currency women understood, one male CEOs didn't know. She leveraged her experience as a woman.

According to Stanford, "Sara Blakely, then 27, was prepping for a party when she realized she didn't have the right undergarment to wear under white pants. To solve the issue, she pulled out a pair of scissors and cut the feet off her pantyhose. Thus, Spanx® was born."[37]

Blakely embodies the definition of resourcefulness. The young entrepreneur leveraged the currency of determination to travel from department store to department store. She boldly sent samples to Oprah Winfrey's stylist. Thanks to Ms. Winfrey's endorsement, Spanx became an overnight sensation.

Although Blakely originally found it difficult to make money in a male-dominated boardroom, she leveraged currency and kept winning. Committed to staying resourceful, she proved when you use the right currency, you will succeed.

Remaining Resourceful

I returned to that cafe with a fistful of euros. I made my purchase friction-free and sat down on a chair outside the cafe. I soaked in the sun while drinking my coffee and eating my chocolate croissant. Although I felt peace, I knew soon enough I'd be in serious pain climbing those mountains.

No worries. That whole trip I never struggled with the currency again. Of course, when I ran low on euros I visited several other ATMs. Wherever my Visa wasn't accepted, I remained resourceful and paid with the correct currency. It turns out cycling in the French Alps requires multiple currencies. A wise person knows which one to use at what time.

Treat others with respect and you will always be wealthy, because your community is your real currency.

—— Bryant McGill

Trait Six: Marketing

Master Storytelling

I didn't keep my French cycling trip a secret. I trained for a year with multiple cycling groups, most often with one near my house called Galena Cycling Club. Before I left the United States, my friends told me to post about my adventure in France.

Each day, I recorded my cycling routes with my Strava app. If you're not familiar, "Strava connects millions of runners, cyclists, hikers, walkers and other active people through the sports they love."[38] Think of it as a social network centered around GPS. It tells you how far, how fast, and how high you climb. It adds to your adventures by including photos, videos, and text, so followers get a fuller and richer story.

In addition to posting in the Strava app, I also shared updates on my social media accounts. Some days I posted breathtaking views. Other days I included details of incredible fails. I authentically shared the highs and the lows as well as the wins and the losses. The comments poured in:

I feel like I'm there with you.
I've always wanted to visit France.
Thanks for the tour. It's beautiful.
I'm inspired to dream bigger.
This is exactly what I needed to hear today.
Keep the updates coming.
I love being along for the ride.

Some people took my posts as an invitation to tell their own story. I'm glad they did because their comments inspired me. I read about their goals, dreams, and obstacles, albeit physical, professional, or emotional. My connected community grew even deeper.

They anticipated the next post and tracked my progress online as I made my way across France. Other people I didn't even know, started following, and posting comments along the way. Although I was alone on the mountain, I didn't feel alone.

Good Stories Sell

E-Minds are master marketers. These entrepreneurs understand that the best products and services won't spread far and wide without a story behind it. The human brain loves stories. We want to close the loop mentally and emotionally. When I shared my story, those who resonated wanted more. The daily photos from my France trip created anticipation of the next adventure I'd experience. People bought into my story, because over time it became their story.

One reader commented, "Just added cycling in France to my bucket list."

Think about this statement. Without any force, someone of their own volition chose to add my adventure to their short list of experiences they want to accomplish before they die. That's significant and it illustrates the power of storytelling.

> ENTREPRENEURS UNDERSTAND THAT THE BEST PRODUCTS AND SERVICES WON'T SPREAD FAR AND WIDE WITHOUT A STORY BEHIND IT.

I know some people dislike social media and I can understand why. There are dangers of course:

Some people get addicted.

Others fall into a comparison trap.

And still others just don't care.

Personally, I've always enjoyed the medium as a way to stay in touch. I like to remain connected to what's going on with people I care about.

As an entrepreneur, I've leveraged these platforms as a way to educate and engage potential customers and clients. Storytelling works! Over the past twenty years, half of our new business came from people who saw our story-styled posts on social media. The other half came from people who heard stories (testimonials) from current clients on social media about what it's like to work with our team.

Donald Miller, author of *Building a StoryBrand* unpacks why storytelling is more important than ever before:

> Without a clear, distinct message, customers will not understand what you can do for them and are unwilling to engage, causing you to lose potential sales, opportunities for customer engagement, and much more. In a world filled with constant, on-demand distractions, it has become near-impossible for business owners to effectively cut through the noise to reach their customers. Story helps because it is a sense-making mechanism. Story formulas put everything in order so the brain doesn't have to work to understand what's going on. Story is the greatest weapon we have to combat noise, because it organizes

> information in such a way that people are compelled to listen.[39]

Use Storytelling to Serve

Not all storytelling styles are equal. One common mistake is making yourself the object of focus. Believe it or not, you're not supposed to be the center of your story. It might sound counterintuitive, but it's true.

I see one of my connections get it wrong all the time. His posts take on a reporter style, focusing on his achievements and adventures. He'll post about what he's eating and where he's going. It feels like he's bragging, but more than anything it's awkward. There's no storyline for people to get onboard. His posts are random, devoid of purpose and his audience is unsure about what action to take—if any. As a result, his engagement is extremely low.

Proper storytelling feels different. It avoids "product pushing." People see through those tactics because it feels manipulative. Effective storytelling focuses on serving, not selling. Your pictures and videos might be the medium, but remember those aren't the message. It's something much bigger than you.

> EFFECTIVE STORYTELLING FOCUSES ON SERVING, NOT SELLING.

In France, my posts centered on transcendent topics like struggle, doubts, and fears. Other times I focused on the joy of effective training or overcoming difficult obstacles—like the mountains in your own life. My posts told a larger story about how we're all being called to an epic adventure if we have the courage to face it head on.

Notice the difference?

One post gets avoided. The other gets engagement. One is about self, the other about serving. I have many friends and clients who do this so well. It's why I consume their content and it's why they keep attracting more followers.

Sure some critics will object, claiming social media is fake. But, despite what you might've heard, I've developed many online friendships that go incredibly deep.

I think about my own business. Although we've never officially "met" many clients in person, we've helped launch their books and optimize their businesses. We've helped other virtual clients protect their intellectual property through our blockchain technology service, Easy IP™.[40] Many of these relationships started with a post, video, or podcast episode.[41] Some have evolved into global collaborations.

You're Not Alone

Remember the first Trait—Independence? Although E-Minds must accept that no one is coming to save them, this doesn't mean they're all alone. Quite the opposite—actually. E-Minds take full ownership, accountability, and responsibility for their successes and failures. But they never forget they exist in community, not in isolation. E-Minds are part of a larger narrative. Proper storytelling cultivates friendships and followers from around the world.

The entrepreneurial journey offers this same promise. Although no one is coming to save you, your story will attract people who want to join you. You'll meet some people who don't have the courage to take the risk you've taken and others who simply aren't able. These like-minded sojourners find your story inspiring and stay engaged because they want to find out how your story ends.

The truth is, they see themselves in your story and they become inextricably linked to your success or failure. They might lack courage, but they see you as courageous. They might lack belief, but see you as believable. They root for you, because it's a vote for their future success.

I tell my author clients to invite their potential readers in, long before they publish their book. This includes sharing details with their audience, taking them into the fun of picking a title or cover, and communicating highs and lows. As they see your story take shape, they feel a sense of ownership. When your book launch day comes around, they jump in to help because they're launching a part of themselves too.

THEY ROOT FOR YOU, BECAUSE IT'S A VOTE FOR THEIR FUTURE SUCCESS.

It reminds me of two pregnant women. Who gets more online engagement? The woman who announces her baby was born yesterday? Or the woman who shares the details about: discovering she's pregnant, choosing the baby's name, announcing the gender, decorating the nursery, picking out the paint, building the crib, and then finally the birth day. You get the point. People want to get caught up in the story.

Author Jeff Goins provides a different spin with a concept he coined, "practicing in public." Goins shares how many geniuses leveraged this secret, including Pablo Picasso. The artist didn't start storytelling until after he became a success. Rather, he showed up with warts and in the beginning he offered to paint one woman in particular, Gertrude Stein.[42] In other words, Picasso invited others into his story while he traveled the road to greatness.

It's not just a principle for painters. Goins continues:

> Comedian Chris Rock has a habit of showing up unannounced to small nightclubs. No one in the audience knows he's coming. They haven't bought a ticket to see him; they aren't even aware of his performance until he's onstage doing it. Often in front of audiences with fewer than 50 people, he takes the stage and goes through a 45-minute routine. Surprisingly, he isn't very good. With a legal notepad in hand, Rock offers the material in an informal and un-exaggerated voice, seeing which jokes connect and which ones fall flat. This is far from the polished, outlandish version we are used to seeing on TV comedy specials. The same goes for Louis C.K. or Steve Martin. This was how musician Beck Hansen began his career, as well, playing for audiences who didn't want to hear folk songs in rock and roll clubs. There is no other way to get good than putting your work out there, sharing it for the whole world to see and hear.[43]

This type of ground-floor storytelling engages audiences and increases awareness. Kickstarter and GoFundMe, two crowdfunding platforms, recognize this reality. Millions of dollars of pre-sales have been generated by inviting people to get in before you go big time. Grassroot strategy works because early adopters take pride in discovering new art and new entrepreneurs.

People Connect to Stories

We remember stories more than data. Psychologist Jerome Bruner says people are twenty-two times more likely to remember a fact when it has been wrapped in a story.[44] It's difficult to argue. *Hidden Figures*, the true story of NASA's Kathleen Johnson was the highest grossing movie at the eighty-ninth Academy Awards. If this movie simply focused on numbers, ticket sales wouldn't have skyrocketed. However, by integrating a story audiences stayed engaged and couldn't help engage in word-of-mouth marketing.

The same can be said about *The Sound of Freedom*, which was released on July 4, 2023. Also a true story, this action-packed film followed a federal agent who rescued children from human trafficking. At the end of the movie, audiences were invited to spread the word by purchasing a ticket for a future anonymous moviegoer. The ticket sales surprised Hollywood and the rest of the world, doubling the per theater revenue of the Indiana Jones movie that was released the same weekend. No one can argue that people love stories about heroes, and in this case, a hero who didn't emerge from a comic book.

When we share our story with passion, people can't help but listen. I saw this pattern in a church planter over twenty years ago. Back when I was a pastor at a church near Columbus, we sponsored a minister named Clancy Cruise. He and his family served out of our church for about six months while they prepared to start a church in Marysville, Ohio.

> WHEN WE SHARE OUR STORY WITH PASSION, PEOPLE CAN'T HELP BUT LISTEN.

Although I only saw Clancy once a week at our Tuesday leadership meeting, I was always deeply impressed. When it was his turn to share, he could have settled on typical number reporting categories: contacts, sermons, visitations, and conversions. However, without fail, he leveraged storytelling nuanced with names and details. He told us fresh tales of transformed lives from the week prior. We all stopped whatever we were doing, intently listening because his stories captured our attention and respect. Giving increased and the new church is growing to this day.

I've always been a sucker for stories. Even as a kid at meal times, I read the origin story off product labels. It turns out my habit isn't isolated. Other than the "Home" page, the second most popular page on a website is the "About" page. Stories transcend cultures and countries because it's part of what makes us human. Everybody craves connection and proper storytelling helps us connect the dots.

There is no greater agony than bearing an untold story inside you.

—Maya Angelou

Trait Seven: Investment

Make Friends Before You Need Them

It's *lonely* at the top.
You *can't* trust anyone.
Success is a *solo* sport.

Some people buy into these negative views of entrepreneurship—casually tossing around toxic platitudes. The good news is these statements don't need to be reality. Thankfully there's an alternative that's also true:

It's *fun* at the top.
You *can* trust people.
Success is a *team* sport.

Chances are somewhere along the way there will be failures, betrayals, and obstacles, but this doesn't mean we need to stay bitter. When my friends bailed on the France trip, I could have "gone dark." It would have been easy for me to pull back and choose isolation. Yet when entrepreneurs settle on going solo, they stunt success.

But wait, you might be thinking? I thought in the beginning of the book we were told to embrace independence? True, but entrepreneurship is a paradox. Consider these two apparent contradictions.

Trait 1: Independence—No one is coming to save you.
Trait 7: Investment—Make friends before you need them.

These two traits coexist. We need both. There's a time to dig deep and battle self. And there's a time to reach out and ask for help.

Many people turn inside when life gets hard. In times of trial, it feels safer to keep to ourselves and stop investing in people. But that's backwards thinking. Of course E-Minds must develop a strong internal core, but they must also cultivate collaborative relationships.

Oftentimes we overcomplicate this step. Don't stress. Friendships can begin with the smallest of efforts. King Solomon said, "A man that hath friends must shew himself friendly."

On my French adventure, because of my language challenges, I found myself even friendlier than usual. I didn't have a choice because I needed help at every turn. After all, I didn't know how to read labels at the store, pay at the checkout line, or even open the front door on my rental.

Making friends before you need them takes relatively little effort. I found myself helping others by offering food or taking a picture for other cyclists who gathered around the sign displaying the respective name and elevation height at the top of the mountain.

My New French Friends

On the second day of my cycling journey, I needed a train to take me to the base of a mountain many miles from the town I was residing. I woke up early and I didn't feel incredibly chatty. Still, I chose to be kind to the other passengers as we waited for the train. I greeted one older couple with a *bonjour*. Turned out the gentleman spoke a little English and so we spoke for a little while. He shared a bit about France and how he traveled once to the United States. I appreciated his demeanor. Little did I know how valuable that five-minute friendship would soon become.

In France, since the trains run fast and tight, they require multiple boarding platforms. Passengers must position themselves on the correct platform each accessed by a different elevator or staircase. Loudspeakers announce arrivals, departures, and changes throughout the station—however, it's all in French. My friends told me the sounds and directions are difficult enough to navigate in French, but as someone who only speaks English, I didn't even try. Instead, I kept checking my train app to stay alert of any changes.

Without any warning my "five-minute friend" grabbed my arm and started pulling me toward an elevator, amidst all the noise. "Hurry!" he said. I followed him and his wife, matching their brisk pace.

Unfortunately, the app didn't update when the train switched platforms. It was soon apparent that I would have missed my train and lost an entire day of cycling had I not made friends before I needed them. I thanked the couple many times for their kindness. They rerouted me to the correct platform despite my language challenges.

Investing in people became a constant theme during my French adventure. I encouraged other cyclists by offering smiles, waves, and nods. Everywhere I went I oozed gratitude and appreciation, never knowing if my positivity would be reciprocated or rejected.

I found the answer when I ran out of water on a couple of climbs. Thankfully, a few people were quick to help.

One afternoon, in a random village, I saw a woman reading a book in front of her house. I apologized for my intrusion, but explained I had run out of water. With a large mountain ahead of me—literally—I had no shame asking for help. Dehydration wasn't a destination I wanted to experience.

She graciously obliged and I offered to pay her. Although she refused money, we chatted for a few minutes, and then I continued on my journey. Every encounter reminded me of this simple, yet imperative, principle: Invest in every person you meet as though they will one day be your partner, collaborator, client, or friend. Give to everyone and expect nothing in return.

> INVEST IN EVERY PERSON YOU MEET AS THOUGH THEY WILL ONE DAY BE YOUR PARTNER, COLLABORATOR, CLIENT, OR FRIEND.

This perspective is so different and that's why it works so well. Embody this mindset and you quickly become an outlier. The reason is that most of us grew up hardwired for competition, not collaboration. Look no further than the old adage, THE EARLY BIRD GETS THE WORM. See if you can relate to this excerpt from my book *Day Job to Dream Job*.

> Usually, a well-meaning adult relayed this story to you to motivate you to action. Innocent? Seemingly. Until you unpack the proposition. Let's focus on the two main characters in this ultra short yet influential story: the worm and the bird. First the worm.[45]

Notice, *the* worm?

As if there's only one worm in the entire world? Last time I checked, billions of worms populated the earth. Grab a shovel and start digging anywhere and you'll find more worms than you ever wanted.

The worm?

Try more than 4,400 species of worms already discovered, classified, and named by scientists![46]

Now, notice the *early* bird.

In our short story, why must birds compete against each other? Can't they form teams or families? Last time I checked, birds live in communities and work toward a common goal.

Besides, early signifies a race. What about the punctual bird who showed up on time? Is it disqualified?

Fast-forward twenty years and examine those children who believed the early bird gets the worm scarcity story. What do you observe in people who retell that story?

You end up with adults who believe:

- They must compete with everyone else for limited resources.
- Fear must drive their attitudes and actions.
- Other people need to lose just so they can win.

E-Minds see the world in a different way. Rather than supporting scarcity they think abundantly. They're focused on collaboration, not competition. E-Minds realize the more true friends they acquire, the more they stack the deck in their favor.

Consider a different story that illustrates the point. One of Aseop's Fables, *The Lion and the Mouse*, which has survived centuries. It goes something like this:

E-MINDS REALIZE THE MORE TRUE FRIENDS THEY ACQUIRE, THE MORE THEY STACK THE DECK IN THEIR FAVOR.

> A mouse accidentally woke a sleeping lion set on killing her. She begged for her little life and convinced the lion to be merciful, claiming she would return the favor and help him someday. Amused, the lion agreed, however he doubted the ability of such a tiny creature to ever be of assistance. Some time later, a hunter's heavy netting fell on the lion immobilizing him. Destined to be mounted on a wall somewhere, the king of the

jungle let out a great roar in protest. The mouse heard the cry and immediately came to the lion's rescue. In no time, his little friend had chewed through the thick ropes and freed the king.

Many see this as a child's bedtime story, however, it's much deeper than that. The truth is that nobody knows when they'll need help. If we stay self-absorbed or hide in pain, we'll never make friends before we need them. However, when we go out of our way to encourage, compliment, and invest in other people, we build a team of allies who line up to help us.

Investing Pays Off

Although I knew no one could climb the mountains for me, I still made it a point to make new friends in France every chance I could. One day I enjoyed a wonderful meal and I sincerely thanked my waitress for the incredible food and service. We talked briefly about the French countryside and local shops. I assumed the brief encounter would be the last time I would ever see her.

However, because my travel plans took a turn (more to come on that), I needed to rent a room. My phone battery nearly died after a full day of cycling and I had less than a 10 percent charge. On those mountains, smart phones provided essential lifelines like navigation and communication. When I asked this waitress if I could borrow a charger she connected me to the kind gentleman who checked me into that hotel. He lent me his charger overnight and I lived to ride another day.

This might sound like a small gesture, but in this quaint town there was nowhere else to purchase a charger. Without their help, I'm not sure what I would have done. But thanks to this waitress and her friend, I was able to safely navigate the mountain with a fully charged phone.

I've seen this play out too many times to count in my entrepreneurial life. This is why I make it a habit to show up filled up and serve other people. Sometimes it's been as simple as writing a review for someone's product or service. Other times, it's promoting their business on my social media platforms. Most of the time it's simply following the Golden Rule—treating others like you want to be treated.

Friends Help Friends

As I mentioned previously, at one point in my entrepreneurial career, we invested up to $50,000 in digital advertising per month. The numbers worked so we kept on paying for lead generation. These days it's different. We don't spend a dime on ads. Instead, we invest in taking care of clients, and as a result, we receive endless referrals.

Three hours ago today, I received another referral via email. The message said this:

It's my pleasure to e-introduce you to one another.

Kary, _____ is a friend who reached out to me via LinkedIn to have a conversation regarding how to grow the distribution and impact of her new book. I think she would be well served by connecting with you, Kary.

Blessings to you both.

Whenever someone connects me, I make it a point to follow up promptly. My goal is to intentionally over deliver and provide exceptional value. I aim to honor the person who made the introduction. After all, this person trusts me and I want to demonstrate that I am trustworthy. I Bcc the original person, thanking them for connecting us and acknowledging their time is precious. I also include a specific compliment, making sure to edify the person in front of their referral. This serves all parties and ensures we're starting the new relationship from a place of appreciation and abundance.

This practice is so ingrained now I recently forgot how it feels to be on the receiving end.

As I mentioned earlier, eighteen years ago I was rejected by Cedarville University when I applied to be a professor.

This past December, I "randomly" attended a small Christmas party hosted by the International Center for Creativity (ICC). The two founders, Jim Stevenson and Tom Balliet invited me as their guest. We had met a few years prior and immediately felt a connection. Our friendship deepened over a mutually shared interest in faith, innovation, and entrepreneurship.

That evening, I found myself sitting with faculty and board members from Cedarville, the same university that rejected me.

Over dinner, one of them, a gentleman named Travis, asked me what I did for a living. I told him about my love for entrepreneurship, marketing, and publishing and my passion to speak, write, and teach on the topic.

His eyes lit up. He told me I should teach at Cedarville University as an adjunct professor. I thanked him kindly, but told him I didn't have the bandwidth since I was running two companies. He promised to connect me with the Dean of the Business School. I thanked him and then forgot about his promise and drove home.

The next morning when I awoke, I found an email from him connecting me to Dr. Jeff Haymond. He told me more than teaching adjunct, they'd been searching the past two years for the right candidate to fill an endowed position, the Berry Chair of Entrepreneurship. The more I listened, the more I got excited. Evidently that love for teaching the next generation had never left me. Still, I told him I must decline. "I am an entrepreneur and I can't give up my businesses."

"Give them up?" he asked. "We don't want you to do that. If you're going to teach entrepreneurship, you need to remain an entrepreneur. It's necessary for you to have credibility with the students!"

I couldn't believe my ears. Rather than viewing my businesses as a distraction, he saw them as a qualification. He also told me in addition to the salary and benefits the position included free tuition for all three of my kids.

Looking back, God sure has a massive sense of humor. Someone once said, "People's rejection is God's protection." How true. Back in 2005, I wasn't ready to teach. And I hadn't yet discovered my love for entrepreneurship. I needed to take a detour on that professor dream and keep growing personally and professionally. I've learned when you prepare for the moment, the moment is prepared for you.

A few weeks after our phone call, I was already teaching my first course as an adjunct professor. I quickly fell in love with the students and the mission of the university. Months later we created a mutually beneficial collaboration, and today, I serve as the Entrepreneurship Chair while running my two companies. I couldn't have crafted a more exciting and fulfilling story. Through the process, I learned that everybody wins when you invest in others and make friends before you need them.

A friend is one soul abiding in two bodies.
—Aristotle.

Trait Eight: Tenacity

Go to the Next Town

I don't typically eat twist ice cream cones.

But here I was, sitting on a chair at the base of the tallest paved mountain in Europe doing just that. I stared at the massive rock in front of me, contemplating on whether or not I should begin the climb. It was my second day of cycling, and I had already climbed Mont Cenis and descended into Italy that morning. Then I turned around, climbed the back of Mont Cenis and cycled the twelve mile valley trek to Bonneval-sur-Arc, where the ascent to Col de l'Iseran began.

Who was I fooling?

Cycling more than sixty miles and climbing over seven thousand feet, I already felt completely exhausted. I didn't know where I'd find the energy to summit the tallest mountain I had ever attempted to climb. The afternoon was mostly gone and the sun was already trying to hide behind some of the mountains. I knew I only had a few hours left of daylight.

"I don't think you should do it," the twentysomething ice cream worker warned. "Not this time of day."

"Yeah, but I have to make it back to my Airbnb tonight," I explained. "I don't want to give up and then travel all of this way again tomorrow."

He just shook his head, shaming me.

Col de l'Iseran is the tallest paved mountain in Europe, and I didn't want to leave France without conquering it. The mountain is feared and for good reason. It's referred to as the "mecca of the Tour de France cycling race."[47] Another website calls it, "The true giant of the Alps." I licked my ice cream cone mechanically, staring straight at the foreboding mountain right in front of me.

DangerousRoads.Org classifies this massive rock with both caution and encouragement:

> Known as the King of the Alps and the holy grail for many motorcycle and bike tourers, the pass is wild, intimidating, lonely and epic. The landscape is desolate, rough and untouched. It will leave you breathless and you must do it."[48]

I wanted to do it, but the odds were against me. I was dead tired, the sun was setting, and even if I made it to the top, I'd have to cycle all the way back to my rental apartment after descending.

"The mountain gets very cold and dark and you don't want to be up there when night falls," the ice cream man explained.

Although I didn't ask for his advice, I knew he was just trying to be helpful. Too bad I didn't have a vehicle, or I would just travel to my Airbnb tonight and then back to l'Iseran tomorrow.

"Why don't you get a hotel here?"

"Nah, I'm going to give it a shot," I said, strapping on my helmet.

Despite his warning, I started my ascent with the goal of conquering Col de l'Iseran. But after the first few hundred meters, I came to my senses.

You know what? He's right.

I hadn't even considered the option of changing my plans and staying at the base of the mountain. Although I didn't have any clothes or toiletries, I had the correct currency and a flexible mindset. So, I biked back to the ice cream man and asked him for a room at Hôtel Le Glacier des Evettes. He told me he had to check with the manager.

I wasn't sure what he meant.

After all, it was his suggestion to stay there. What did he mean he had to check? I started to get a little nervous. A few minutes later he reappeared with bad news. "Sorry, all the rooms are full."

It turns out the little town was hosting a large motorcycle event. Now empathetic, the ice cream man pointed me to a small inn called Auberge d'Oul just down the road, but still within the village. Unfortunately, it was also full. The people there recommended I travel to one town back and try my luck there.

A FEW MINUTES LATER HE REAPPEARED WITH BAD NEWS. "SORRY, ALL THE ROOMS ARE FULL."

The closest village was a few miles toward the direction of Mont Cenis. Normally, I hate backtracking, but it was the best option I had. The two inns didn't have any rooms either. Soon, I was four towns back from Col de l'Iseran and still had no place to stay for the night. I knew if I didn't find a hotel soon, I would need to return to Modane so I could catch the train. From there I'd have to pedal hard to arrive at my Airbnb—hopefully before sunset.

I felt my chances of conquering Col de l'Iseran slipping away. I hated that feeling.

Keep the Goal. Adjust the Plan.

E-Minds find a way to win. They're tenacious. Rather than surrendering, they simply go to the next town.

"Yes, sir, we have one room left. It will be sixty-one euros."

You can imagine my excitement when I heard the news.

"And if you'd like a steak dinner and a breakfast buffet with the room, it will be ninety-nine euros."

"Seriously!" I said. "You're awesome. I'll take it."

Thankfully, this hotel took Visa. I asked the host where I could buy toiletries and a pair of shorts. He pointed to a place across the street. I carried my bicycle up the staircase and checked into my room. Then I headed to the store to make a few purchases. I wasn't about to wear my cycling shorts to a fancy steak dinner.

I had one goal—to climb the highest paved road in Europe on my bicycle. As I entered that fifth town from Col de l'Iseran, still hoping I'd find a room, I thought about tenacity. Although I didn't know *how* I'd succeed, I knew I *would* succeed. Quitting certainly wasn't an option.

I learned a powerful truth many years ago:

Successful entrepreneurs *keep the goal*, but adjust the plan.
Unsuccessful entrepreneurs *keep the plan*, but adjust the goal.

I almost slipped and lost my focus. I almost kept my plan—returning to my Airbnb—rather than keeping my goal—climbing Col de l'Iseran. Thankfully, the ice cream man gave me an idea I hadn't considered. Once I woke up to that reality, I realized many more options existed. At that moment, everything changed because I tapped into Trait 8: Tenacity. I knew I'd find a way to win, even if it meant sleeping under the stars.

E-Minds prepare for the unexpected. They realize launches won't go right, products will get delayed, people will let you down, affiliates won't show up, and ads will get rejected. Despite all of this, they still find a way to win. They simply "go to the next town." Sometimes, it's just a metaphor. Other times, entrepreneurs literally need to knock on more doors.

Either way, tenacity takes us to the "next town." Too often we stay stuck in our current location. I remember early on in my career trying to convince all the people around me about my big dreams. Most people didn't support me. They weren't rude or ill willed. They just couldn't see what I saw. I felt crushed because I didn't think they believed in me. The truth is—at that point—I didn't believe in myself. I needed to grow into a bigger person and I needed to leave my comfort zone to do so.

E-Minds keep moving forward. The will to win pushes us to the next town because we need a new space to thrive. Many times it's not our product or marketing, it's that we just haven't found the right location yet.

There's a powerful story on this topic that went viral a few years ago:

> A bottle of water at Costco is approximately $0.25.
> The same bottle in the supermarket is worth about $0.50.
> The same bottle in a bar costs $2.
> In a good restaurant or hotel, it can be worth up to $3.
> At an airport or on the plane, you may be charged $5.

> **The bottle and the brand are the same, the only thing that changes is the place.**
> Each place gives a different value to the same product.
> When you feel like you are worth nothing and everyone around you belittles you, change places, do not stay there.
> Have the courage to change places and go to a place where
> you are given the value you deserve.
> Surround yourself with people who really appreciate your worth.
> Don't settle for less.[49]

I love that line. *The bottle and the brand are the same, the only thing that changes is the place.* Sometimes people aren't willing to pay for the value we create in the world. In those scenarios, it's not because our product or service is wrong. Rather, it's because the environment is wrong. You can have the best solution in the world, but if the room is full of wrong fit clients, it doesn't matter what you do.

Early on in my career I was stuck trying to serve the wrong people. Other times my value wasn't recognized. We can give up and quit like many entrepreneurs do. Or we can rise up, tap into tenacity, and go to the next town.

IN THOSE SCENARIOS, IT'S NOT BECAUSE OUR PRODUCT OR SERVICE IS WRONG. RATHER, IT'S BECAUSE THE ENVIRONMENT IS WRONG.

The Triumph of Tenacity

I loved my stay at the Hotel la Vieille Poste. The kind host let me borrow his phone charger so I could start the next day on a full charge. That night, I feasted on an amazing steak dinner with incredible sides and a scrumptious dessert. After my meal, I climbed the staircase, brushed my teeth, and fell asleep the minute my head hit the pillow.

The next morning, I woke up refreshed and ready to go. I ate one of the best breakfasts of my life and then stuffed my new shorts into my back jersey pocket. I rode back to the base of Col de l'Iseran with a surge of energy and a debt of gratitude to the ice cream man who had served me up such a wonderful idea. Although his hotel was full, he reminded me of my goal. And once I refocused my brain, I tapped into tenacity and found a way forward.

I summited l'Iseran several hours later and took in the beauty. On the top of the mountain I saw a small stone chapel called Chapelle Notre-Dame-de-Toute-Prudence. Although it was the middle of summer, I was surrounded by rock and snow. It felt otherworldly.

At some point in summiting the mountain, my prescription sunglasses fell out of my back jersey pocket. Although I was aware a brand new pair back home would cost me a couple of hundred dollars, amidst all the beauty that surrounded me I didn't let frustration get the best of me. After all, I had conquered the mountain that almost conquered me.

I descended the mountain and then headed back to Saint Jean de Maurienne. I ended up buying a cheap pair of replacement sunglasses to get me through the rest of the trip. I've learned to roll with the punches throughout my entrepreneurial journey. I've realized you'll have wins and losses, as well as opened doors and closed doors. You might even have to replace a few pairs of sunglasses along the way.

Bottom line, it's all about tenacity. If you adjust the plan and keep the goal, then most of the time you'll end up on top. And in this particular case, ending on "top" meant reaching the highest paved road in Europe.

Let me tell you the secret that has led me to my goal. My strength lies solely in my tenacity.

—Louis Pasteur

Trait Nine: Intuition

Lean into the Curve

When I descended the first mountain on my first day of cycling, I definitely felt out of my comfort zone. I followed my new French friend from a distance, watching him fly down those hairpins effortlessly. He grew up on these mountains—literally—and he knew them well, clearly conquering any lingering fears he might have had decades ago.

Me on the other hand, I gripped my brakes as if my life depended on it, because in my mind it did. I felt awkward and I'm sure I looked awkward, fighting gravity the whole way down. My forearms hurt from excessive braking and once I even pulled over to shake out my arms. My descent took a ridiculous amount of time, but I managed to meet my French friend in one piece at the bottom of the mountain.

Although we couldn't communicate with words, he used body language to demonstrate a leaning position. Interpreting his motions, I assumed he was encouraging me to lean into the curve on my next mountain.

How far can you go?

Before I left the United States, some people asked me how *far* I planned on riding while in France. I didn't know the correct answer, but I quickly learned that this was the wrong question. The better question is how *high* I planned on climbing.

In the French Alps, *distance* is of little importance. *Elevation*—on the other hand—is of extreme importance. During my first day of cycling, I climbed nearly eleven thousand five hundred feet. That was the day I conquered Col Du Mollard, Col de la

Croix de Fer, Col du Glandon, Col du Chaussy and Les Lacets de Montvernier.

At the end of the day, I felt great because I had trained hard. However, as I was all alone on the mountain the following day, I had an interesting thought. I wonder if I could climb fifteen thousand feet in one day?

Different types of people ask different types of questions. This is why it's so important you associate with people who match the size of your dreams. I like to associate with people who dream big, like my coach Dan Sullivan.

DIFFERENT TYPES OF PEOPLE ASK DIFFERENT TYPES OF QUESTIONS. THIS IS WHY IT'S SO IMPORTANT YOU ASSOCIATE WITH PEOPLE WHO MATCH THE SIZE OF YOUR DREAMS.

He tells a story about confronting a powerful question when he was a young boy:

> One February when I was about eleven years old, I was walking through the cornfields. It was that time of year when it's usually still very cold in the Midwest. It was a very clear day, very sunny, without one cloud in the sky. You could even see the moon starting to come up.
>
> I remember the crunch of the snow under my boots, a sound I always liked. Of course, everything had long been harvested, but you could follow the rows of cornstalk stubble just like you were following a path. One of the great things about walking through the bare fields in winter was the clear view of the planes that regularly flew overhead.

On this particular February day, I heard a plane coming and knew it was a four-propeller DC-6. I watched it, trying to figure out which airline it was, but it was hard to see in the bright sun. All of a sudden, just like an electric shock, a thought came to me: I wonder how far I can go.

It was just a question, but I remember it felt the way others have described religious or spiritual experiences. Looking back at that moment, I knew I had discovered my purpose in life. I recall having a feeling of connection—of being connected to this question, which became dominant in my thinking and my life.

How far can I go?[50]

I love Dan's question. E-Minds ask questions other people don't ask. They wonder about things other people don't even think about. This doesn't make them better or worse. It just makes them different.

Look at human innovation. The reason we experience breakthroughs in technology is because certain people asked interesting questions.

I believe from a young age most of us ask interesting questions. Hang out with a child and you will hear the wonder in their voice. But somewhere along the way on our path toward adulthood, we stop wondering and we also stop asking questions.

The inventors of yesterday and the entrepreneurs of today both have something in common. They never stop wondering or asking questions. As a result, they tap into a different set of answers that propel their thinking to new heights.

Monster Day

After I asked the question if I could climb fifteen thousand feet in one day, I knew I had to try it. Somewhere in my mind, the possibility of accomplishing my goal already existed and I knew I'd be unsatisfied unless I tried. So I targeted my last day of cycling as the ideal day to give it a shot.

THE INVENTORS OF YESTERDAY AND THE ENTREPRENEURS OF TODAY BOTH HAVE SOMETHING IN COMMON. THEY NEVER STOP WONDERING OR ASKING QUESTIONS.

I made preparations, mapping out the route the night before with an online tool called Ride with GPS. I figured it would probably take me around eleven-hours and include clocking over one hundred miles of distance and 15,000 feet of elevation. To do this, I'd have to start very early and limit my breaks, waking up before dawn and taking a train from Saint Jean de Maurienne to Saint Michel de Maurienne. From there, I would begin climbing and not stop climbing until dark.

In order to reach that elevation, I would need to summit seven peaks including Col de Télégraphe, Col du Galibier, and Col du Lautaret. After those three, I would attempt the infamous Col du Granon, a climb which was said to have cracked the two-time Tour de France champion Tadej Pogačar in 2022[51]. Some say he spent too much energy on Galibier and Lautaret, but whatever the reason, Col du Granon was the turning point in the most famous cycling tour that year. Tour de France champion Jonas Vingegaard had a few thoughts regarding that particular climb:

> On the Col du Granon, I tried to make the race as hard as possible. That col is a beast of a climb. Incredibly tough. I don't think I know or have ever conquered a tougher climb as a finish col. I gave everything until the finish. Not only was it my first stage win in the Tour, but it also gave me my first yellow jersey. A day I will never forget.

Despite knowing that even top performers find Granon to be the second most difficult in the Briancon region, and the sixth toughest climb in all of France, I was determined to make it to the top. Then once I reached the top, I would only be halfway done with my day. I would then turn around and summit the backside of Col du Lautaret, Col du Galibier, and Col du Télégraphe all with enough speed and time to catch the train by 8:00 PM.

Crazy? Of course. But, in my gut I thought it *might* work. Based upon the mileage, the watts, the daylight, and the elevation, it *should* work, that is if nothing went wrong. Only time would tell.

The first part of the day went perfectly. I climbed the first three mountains and then stopped for a quick omelet, the biggest omelet I'd ever eaten. It was lunchtime and I needed the protein. I asked the waitress to bring out my check with the food, so I could eat quickly and avoid wasting any daylight.

I finally reached the base of Col du Granon in the early afternoon. I called Chet and told him I was going to dedicate the climb to him and his wife. It turned out she was having surgery on that exact day during that exact climb. For nearly two hours, I stood up, pedaling in my "granny gear" one stroke after another. I prayed for Chet and his wife during the entire climb since I needed something for my mind to focus on instead of the physical pain.

The summer sun beat down causing sweat to pour off my forehead. I removed my new sunglasses so I could wipe my face with my glove every minute or two. I only went as fast as necessary to keep my bicycle upright. By far, it was the most difficult climb I ever did. When I reached the top, I took a moment to catch my breath. Then I purchased a couple of bottles of sparkling water, drank them immediately, and asked for a refill on my water bottles.

I left Chet a voice text and told him I reached the top and that I would keep praying until I heard otherwise. A minute later, I descended down this highest category (HC) mountain, realizing I had three more mountains to climb before my train departed at 8 PM. I kept riding all afternoon, the sun descending faster and faster behind the towering rock. When I reached the top of the final mountain, Col du Galibier, the wind whipped unforgivingly. The roads that hosted sporadic cyclists throughout the day were now completely abandoned.

I learned a tough lesson on that trip, why cyclists pack windbreakers. After an intense climb, you're covered in sweat. However, many of these mountains are tall enough to host snow throughout much of the summer. The moment you start descending, all that sweat freezes. The brisk wind pierces through your clothing. Even in July, cyclists have been treated for hypothermia during the Tour de France.[52] Windbreakers can provide protection because they're light enough to pack in your jersey pocket, but they also keep you warm as you reach incredibly fast speeds on the descent.

Unfortunately, I didn't pack one so instead, I just told my mind to embrace the cold. My body was having none of it. I shook the whole way down, fingers freezing and teeth chattering. Although my short sleeve jersey provided little warmth, I focused instead on the train departure time and maintaining a good cadence so I could still catch it.

I made it a point to stay mentally engaged since I still had to be extremely careful going downhill at such high speeds without a guardrail. I felt a few moments of anxiety especially on those occasions when a car passed me on the narrow road and pushed me closer to the edge of the cliff.

Lean Into the Curve

The night before, Chet texted me and told me to try his favorite restaurant. Unfortunately it was closed, so I tried a different one instead. Although the atmosphere was average, the food was the best I had found in France. Italian themed, the Restaurant-pizzeria Chez Deniz, served incredible goat cheese salad and flatbread pizza with hot chili sauce. I topped off my dinner with an addictive dessert—warm raisin bread with cool ice cream.

Hungry and cold, nearing the end of my final day of cycling, I locked onto the concept of food, realizing I could catch a late dinner back at that same restaurant if I made the 8 PM train.

Time kept slipping and the sun kept fading. It would be close. Although the final miles were all downhill, when you're thousands of feet above sea level, long descents take time. I remembered what my French friend told me with his body language: lean into the curve. I figured what the heck and so I put his advice into practice and accentuated each hairpin, leaning hard into the curve.

He was right!

This technique made the ride much faster and upon further research, much safer too. I discovered days after my descent that the centrifugal force of the turn causes an imbalance and pushes the bicycle outward. Leaning into the curve allows you to counteract the centrifugal force by creating an inward torque that counteracts gravity. The faster you go, the more you need to lean. At first it feels counterintuitive, but the more you practice, the more familiar it feels and the faster you can accelerate. By my final day I gained the competence and confidence to lean into the curve.

Like cycling, leaning into the curve for entrepreneurs takes practice too. In my book *The Deeper Path*, I share about a related process I call The Deeper Path Payoff™. It all starts with clarity. Once we achieve it, then competence and confidence kick in. The process look like this:

Clarity ⇒ Competence ⇒ Confidence

Anytime we begin anything new we're not quite sure what to do. Take cycling. No matter how much I trained in Ohio, nothing could prepare me for the French Alps. But as the miles kept coming, the process became clearer. By putting it into practice I gained competence. This competence grew into confidence.

This is the path for mastering any skill.

By experiencing clarity, competence, and confidence, we can trust our gut in greater ways. By listening to our intuition we can start having more fun. E-Minds trust their intuition. They lean into the curve as counterintuitive as it might feel at first.

BY EXPERIENCING CLARITY, COMPETENCE, AND CONFIDENCE, WE CAN TRUST OUR GUT IN GREATER WAYS.

There's nothing wrong with CEOs who have a big board of directors. But for E-Minds, it's often just us and the mountain in front of us. We see the obstacles in front of us and we must engage our brains. But thinking like an entrepreneur also requires action. We see trends and lean into them. We sense market shifts and we must adjust accordingly.

Each connection and data point provide more clarity. By leveraging this clarity, we then have the courage to move and act and risk. As we do, we gain competence and eventually confidence. This is the path all successful entrepreneurs take.

We can see it in the example of Elon Musk and SpaceX as they reimagined the rocket industry. At first, SpaceX was simply going to buy pre-built rockets, a costly endeavor. But fueled by intuition, Elon studied the individual components that make up rockets. He called this process "thinking from first principles."[53] This unique perspective helped him realize how SpaceX could build them cheaper by purchasing the pieces and parts separately.

Inexpensive rockets meant more launches and more data leading to faster prototypes. His intuition changed the entire industry.

Leaning into your intuition gives you an advantage. It's not guessing. It's guiding. And it only works when you've built up an incredible amount of inner trust. Intuition allows you to flex your entrepreneurial muscles—not in an arrogant way, but in an utilitarian way.

If you're great at relationships—lean into them.
If you excel at speaking on a stage, lean into it.
If writing or product development is your strength,
lean into it.
The more you lean into the curve, the more confidence
you'll have.

As I leaned into the curves heading back to the train, I got faster and faster. With each mile, I shaved seconds off my time. And by the time I reached the bottom of Col du Télégraphe, I felt alive and on fire, adrenaline pumping.

I made it to St. Michel de Maurienne a few minutes ahead of schedule thanks to the clarity, competence and confidence my French friend had given me. On my final day of cycling, I now understood the concept of leaning into the curve much better than my first day.

I took those curves tentatively on day one, feeling intimidated I would swing way out and ride the brakes the whole way down. I avoided leaning too much because I didn't want to fall over. Logic told me to go slow and stay upright. I've since learned it's actually more dangerous because you're basically flirting with gravity, not to mention wasting time.

I'm grateful for the Frenchman who served as my truth teller. As I started to adopt his technique, I gained confidence as well as speed. The E-Mind works similarly. By listening to successful people around us we can learn their skills. And by practicing those skills, we can grow more confident.

Believe in Yourself

At the beginning of new ventures, most entrepreneurs doubt themselves. We question our plan and wonder if we have what it takes.

In 1954, no one had heard of Johnny Cash, and gospel music was topping the charts. The young unknown walked into Sun Records and sang a song he'd sung dozens of times—a song every singer had sung dozens of times. Johnny Cash did what seemed safe. But like my trip down Col du Télégraphe, what seemed safe was really dangerous.

The label owner, Sam Phillips, only let Cash sing for thirty seconds before shutting him down with a searing statement.

"I don't believe you," Phillips warned.

When Johnny insisted he should finish, Phillips told him nobody wanted to hear a safe gospel song. "It ain't got nothin' to do with believin' in God, Mr. Cash. It has to do with believin' in yourself."[54]

Silence.

Nobody spoke. Nobody moved. Even time stood still.

Then after a few seconds of introspection, Johnny dug deep and began singing a song he'd written while he was serving in the Air Force—a song he believed in.

Sometimes we have to believe in ourselves and trust our gut even when no one else does. Steve Jobs faced humiliation when the board of his own start-up fired him. He risked embarrassment by sticking to what he believed in, and eleven years later, Apple realized their mistake and brought him back.

Those eleven years weren't wasted. That whole time Steve Jobs kept trusting his gut and following his intuition. He invented more products people wanted and even started a company called NeXt, which brought life back to Apple, as well as Pixar®, the world's most successful animation company.[55]

> SOMETIMES WE HAVE TO BELIEVE IN OURSELVES AND TRUST OUR GUT EVEN WHEN NO ONE ELSE DOES.

When we believe in ourselves, trust our intuition, and develop confidence, other people notice. In that moment we flip the script and in the words of my coach Dan Sullivan we become the buyer rather than the seller. It might feel foreign at first, but the more we lean in, the more natural it becomes and the more fun we experience.

Intuition is a very powerful thing, more powerful than intellect.
—Steve Jobs

Trait Ten: Freedom

Order Dessert and Eat it Too

I sat on the patio in the glow of the outdoor lighting. The cool wind blew through the European summer night. I hopped off the train and rode to my new favorite restaurant, still wearing my cycling shorts and jersey. Relaxing in the comfortable chair, I removed my helmet and gloves, endorphins still pumping through my body.

I selected the same exact meal that I ordered the night before, the one I had thought about the whole way up the Col du Galibier. After climbing more than fifteen thousand feet and riding more than one hundred miles, I craved some serious calories.

The goat cheese salad and flatbread pizza with hot chili sauce were even better than I remembered. No holding back for me. After all, I had just completed the adventure of a lifetime.

Reward Yourself

Early in my entrepreneurial career, I hustled all the time. I guess I felt guilty about the thought of resting, like if I stopped to catch my breath I'd somehow lose my edge. I didn't reward myself because it seemed unnecessary or perhaps even wreckless.

How sad.

The good news is I've since changed my thoughts and actions. These days I enjoy celebrating. I know if I don't, I'll wear out myself and my team. No one wants to work with people who fail—or forget—to have fun.

Just look at sports teams and locker room celebrations that leak out onto social media. It's energizing seeing these serious athletes dancing without a care in the world. My favorite thing is watching coaches get into the hype. Often stoic, these coaches break the mold and step into the celebration circle surrounded by a group of athletes cheering them on.

> NO ONE WANTS TO WORK WITH PEOPLE WHO FAIL—OR FORGET—TO HAVE FUN.

Smiles. Laughs. Clapping. Stomping. The culture is electric.

There's a time to "let your hair down," even for bald guys like me.

Humans weren't designed to hustle non-stop because everyone needs down time. Even God rested on the seventh day.

Imagine my cycling adventure if I'd never been able to go downhill. Though that seems ludicrous, entrepreneurs are notorious for continually cycling uphill in their business with no breaks or "down time." These entrepreneurs let their tyrannical schedules sabotage healthy eating and sleeping habits.

Self-care is imperative. Your first priority as an entrepreneur should be maintaining your health. Other team members take their cues from you. Give yourself permission to eat well, exercise often, and enjoy rest. Although it sounds counterintuitive, you and your team will increase productivity by eating, sleeping, and resting well. Over-exertion prevents you from getting into flow.

In my book *Unhackable,* I discuss the advantage of getting into flow, the optimal state of human performance. Within a flow cycle ideas and energy increase. We become 500 percent more productive and lose sense of time and space.[56]

Based on the research of Harvard cardiologist Herbert Benson, there are four stages in the flow cycle: struggle, release, flow, and recovery.[57] Most entrepreneurs ignore the fourth stage: recovery. But without proper rest and relaxation, we rob ourselves from getting into the next flow cycle. This is a classic flaw for many entrepreneurs, myself included. I excel at the first three stages, but that fourth one is easy to overlook.

This is why on my alpine adventure I made it a point to stay hydrated. I kept protein bars and LMNT salt packets in my jersey. And I intentionally scheduled evening meals that forced me to slow down and sit still. The French are experts at turning meals into experiences that often takes quite a bit of time. In fact, they've developed this into a fine art.

E-Minds are wise to adopt this practice for themselves and their teams. Doing so creates more freedom. In my two companies, we inject a huge amount of freedom into our culture. Our people are empowered to set their own schedules. This autonomy fuels freedom. If they need to cut out in the middle of the day and support their children at school functions, no problem. If they need to take off and go hiking—no problem. They know their tasks that need to get done and we trust them to do it.

During my cycling adventure, I was intentional about stopping and smelling the roses—or at least taking pictures of them. Imagine riding the Alps with all those beautiful views and never capturing them. Even on my monster day of fifteen thousand feet of climbing, I still stopped occasionally to breathe in the beauty.

We need to do the same on our entrepreneurial journey. Enjoying the adventure makes the mountaintops that much grander. And even the valleys have their purpose too. At the bottom of those valleys I soaked in the scenery and stumbled upon wildlife as well as rushing rivers.

Don't Skip the Sweets

Back in my home country I don't have dessert too often. I skip sugar and save sweets for special occasions. But after burning thousands and thousands of calories climbing some of the toughest mountains in the world, I intentionally ordered dessert that night—and pretty much at every meal in France. I selected the warm raisin bread with the cool ice cream since it was so tasty the night before.

On topic, entrepreneurs shouldn't feel guilty about eating the fruit of their labor. (Or in our illustration dessert, not fruit.) Some entrepreneurs don't take a regular paycheck when they begin. Others skip vacations for years. I get it, and in the past, I've opted out too. But there's a time to leverage the freedom the E-Mind provides. You don't get awards for always grinding.

> YOU DON'T GET AWARDS FOR ALWAYS GRINDING.

Quite the opposite actually. Rewarding yourself and your team sets up for even more success. It gives you all something to look forward to. Each time you reach a summit, make sure to include a special experience in your agenda. Take a couple of days away with your spouse or friend. Get the best seats in the house. Pay for the upgrade and enjoy the excursions. The point is to infuse a little bit of freedom into the formula. Doing so will create powerful memories and keep you coming back for more.

Do me one favor though. Don't just order that decadent dessert—make sure to eat it too.

Being rich is having money; being wealthy is having time.
—Margaret Bonnano

PART 3

TREK

Gain an Exponential Advantage

"Why should we hire you for the Chair of Entrepreneurship at our university?" the man in the suit asked me with a sincere tone in his voice. "I thought entrepreneurs were notorious for dropping out of college."

I sat in a beautiful wood paneled office, surrounded by hundreds of books. This was my final interview in a series of many interviews. I had waited eighteen years for this opportunity and now the opportunity had come knocking on my door. The Berry Family had created an endowed position and I was only one interview away from making my dream a reality. Rather than being distracted by nerves or anxiety, I tapped into the E-Mind.

"I believe everybody needs to think like an entrepreneur," I replied calmly. "Today's marketplace demands it. We're all brands and businesses. The only real question is, will we take this responsibility seriously?"

We continued an engaging chat about how entrepreneurs benefit from college in ways that transcend degrees and diplomas. I shared how college helped me in my own journey and how it helped many other successful entrepreneurs in my network. Then we switched topics and unpacked what thinking like an entrepreneur means for every student on campus.

WE'RE ALL BRANDS AND BUSINESSES. THE ONLY REAL QUESTION IS, WILL WE TAKE THIS RESPONSIBILITY SERIOUSLY?"

I liked the way he thought and based upon the fact that they hired me, I believe he liked my angle too. Although this university currently only has a minor in entrepreneurship, there's a strategic plan on the table to make it a major in just a few semesters from now.

Even before the summer ended, I met with a small group of students who are passionate about entrepreneurship. Without much direction from me, they created a student org called CUE which stands for Cedarville University Entrepreneurship.

They meet weekly in small groups, creating micro businesses which solve real problems. Their custom cream T-shirts include a CUE logo on the front and a compelling statement on the back:

Entrepreneurship is a mindset, not a minor.

These students inspire me with their engagement and commitment. I feel their fire and desire to create true value. I have hope for the future knowing they're in the game and not sitting on the bench.

The faculty on this campus has been incredibly collaborative too. They've invited me to guest lecture on the topic of entrepreneurship, within multiple courses and majors. Students from all different backgrounds show up filled up, interested in exploring the idea of personal brands and businesses. Whether it's engineering students or music majors, I've been impressed by their energy and openness to wrestle with how thinking like an entrepreneur integrates with their discipline of choice.

A Trek with High Stakes

The truth is our world is changing. If you don't believe me, just reread Peter Diamandis' foreword at the beginning of this book. We have a choice to fight the change or fuel the change and it all comes down to the way we think.

My goal with this book isn't to tell you it's going to be easy. It's actually quite the opposite. In a way it's similar to my French cycling adventure involving mountains and obstacles and goals I wasn't sure I could accomplish. I should probably refer to that adventure as more of a trek. The dictionary defines trek as a long, arduous journey, often over rough terrain. That describes our future world well. The entrepreneurial life isn't an easy one. If someone tries to tell you it is, they're either lying or trying to sell you something.

Let's be honest. These days, life is hard. Pretending it isn't doesn't serve anybody. In fact, I think it harms people because it sets us up for disappointment. This is why I'm so passionate about the E-Mind. Unless we change the way we think, we're going to be in a world of hurt—literally. By choosing "hard," our lives will become easier. But if we choose easy, then our lives will be hard—much harder.

E-Minds believe in a different way and a different world. Applying these Ten Traits prepares anyone in any field for an exponential advantage:

1. **Independence**: No One Is Coming To Save You
2. **Flexibility**: Map It Out, Then Make It Up
3. **Risk**: Embarrassment Is Your Ally
4. **Teachability**: Learn the Language and Culture
5. **Resourcefulness**: Leverage the Correct Currency
6. **Marketing**: Master Storytelling
7. **Investment**: Make Friends Before You Need Them
8. **Tenacity**: Go to the Next Town
9. **Intuition**: Lean into the Curve
10. **Freedom**: Order Dessert and Eat it Too

Consider the alternative. Try living in a world run by people who embrace the exact opposite. That doesn't sound like a reasonable alternative to me. Instead of independence, imagine a life of dependence. Instead of flexibility imagine a world full of obstinance. Rather than freedom, imagine a life of slavery.

No, thank you.

The stakes are high—much higher than they've ever been.

For this reason I'm not asking you to become an entrepreneur.

I'm only asking you to *think* like one.

The E-Mind™

Think like an entrepreneur and gain an exponential advantage starting today.

Col de l'Iseran. 9,068 feet.
The highest paved pass in the Alps.

Appendices

Notes

1. Lewis Howes, "Make These Smart Money Moves Today & Design Your Ideal Life with Gino Wickman" in *School of Greatness* podcast, episode 1225, https://lewishowes.com/podcast/make-these-smart-money-moves-today-design-your-ideal-life-with-gino-wickman/.

2. Ying Lin, "10 Entrepreneur Statistics you Need to Know in 2023,"*Oberlo, January 28, 2023,* https://www.oberlo.com/blog/entrepreneur-statistics.

3. Tom Peters, "The Brand Called You," *Fast Company,* August 31, 1997, https://www.fastcompany.com/28905/brand-called-you.

4. Matthew 5:13-16, New International Version.

5. Matthew 25:24-30, New King James Version.

6. Jill Avery and Rachel Greenwald, "A New Approach to Building Your Personal Brand," *Harvard Business Review,* May-June, 2003, https://hbr.org/2023/05/a-new-approach-to-building-your-personal-brand.

7. 1 Timothy 4:12, NIV.

8. Peters, *Fast Company*.

9. Strategic Coach®, *Who Not How,* https://whonothow.com/.

10. Shopify, "What Is Entrepreneurship? How To Get Started in 2023," June 9, 2023, https://www.shopify.com/blog/what-is-entrepreneurship#.

11. Investopedia, "What Are Intrapreneurs? History, Role, and Benefits for a Company," updated June 29, 2023, https://www.investopedia.com/terms/i/intrapreneur.asp.

12. Coursera, "What Is an Intrapreneur? Definition, Examples, and More," updated June 15, 2023, https://www.coursera.org/articles/intrapreneur.

13. Wallstreetmojo Team, "Intrapreneur," reviewed by Dheeraj Vaidya, accessed October 27, 2023, https://www.wallstreetmojo.com/intrapreneur/.

14. Paul Chamberlain, "Knowledge is not everything," *Taylor & Francis Online*, March 5, 2020, https://doi.org/10.1080/24735132.2020.1731203.

15. Eric Hoffer, "In times of change, learners inherit the earth," *Goodreads*, accessed October 23, 2023, https://www.goodreads.com/quotes/10562-in-times-of-change-learners-inherit-the-earth-while-the.

16. Alpha Ninja, "What Do The Mountain Categories Mean in The Tour de France?" *SLO Cyclist*, July 12, 2016, http://slocyclist.com/what-do-the-mountain-categories-mean-in-the-tour-de-france/.

17. Albert Einstein, "There are two ways to live," *BrainyQuote*, accessed October 27, 2023. https://www.brainyquote.com/quotes/albert_einstein_390808.

18. Hebrews 11:6, NIV.

19. I realize this brings up theological issues like God knowing the future and the impossibility of God truly taking a risk. Nonetheless, that's not the focus of this book or the point I'm making.

20. "Your Brain Performs Better When It Slows Down, with Steven Kotler," *Big Think*, November 4, 2014, https://bigthink.com/surprising-science/steven-kotler-flow-states/.

21. Erin McCarthy, "Roosevelt's 'The Man in the Arena,'" *Mental Floss*, April 23, 2015, https://www.mentalfloss.com/article/63389/roosevelts-man-arena.

22. Gran Fondo Guide, "Top Ten Craziest Switchback Cycle Climbs in the World," accessed October 27, 2023, https://www.granfondoguide.com/Contents/Index/3385/top-ten-craziest-switchbacked-climbs.

23. Tamara Hinson and Jeff Bogle, "18 of the Most Dangerous Roads in the World," *Reader's Digest*, updated January 19, 2023, https://www.rd.com/list/most-dangerous-roads.

24. The Economist, "Entrepreneurship," April 27, 2009, https://www.economist.com/news/2009/04/27/entrepreneurship.

25. Andrew Beattie, "Who Coined the Term 'Entrepreneur'?" *Investopedia,* updated December 28, 2022, https://www.investopedia.com/ask/answers/08/origin-of-entrepreneur.asp#citation-1.

26. Richard Watson, "The Timeline of Failed Predictions, Part 1," *Fast Company,* December 1, 2010, https://www.fastcompany.com/1706712/timeline-failed-predictions-part-1#.

27. Nick Saint, "If You're Not Embarrassed By The First Version Of Your Product, You've Launched Too Late," *Insider*, November 13, 2009. https://www.businessinsider.com/the-iterate-fast-and-release-often-philosophy-of-entrepreneurship-2009-11.

28. Seth Godin, "Polishing perfect," *Seth's Blog,* June 11, 2013, https://seths.blog/2013/06/polishing-perfect.

29. Luke 14:28-32, NIV.

30. Neal DeRidder, "Why are the French afraid of air conditioning?" *Oui in France,* July 20, 2023, https://www.ouiinfrance.com/why-are-the-french-afraid-of-air-conditioning/.

31. Nassie Angadi, "Why is there never any air conditioning in France?" *Snippets of Paris,* accessed October 27, 2023, https://snippetsofparis.com/air-conditioning-france/.

32. 1 Corinthians 9:20-22, NIV.

33. *Dictionary.com,* https://www.dictionary.com/browse/currency, s.v."currency."

34. Iryna Viter, "What is Resourcefulness? Meaning, Examples & Importance," *Runn,* April 15, 2022, https://www.runn.io/blog/what-is-resourcefulness.

35. M. J. Stephy, "Top 10 Memorable Debate Moments: Bush Sr.'s Infamous Gesture," *Time,* accessed October 27, 2023, https://content.time.com/time/specials/packages/article/0,28804,1844704_1844706_1844771,00.html.

36. Allie Nelson, "No Need to Work '9 to 5'—Dolly Parton's Net Worth In 2023 Is Fit for a Country Queen," *Parade,* September 20, 2023, https://parade.com/celebrities/dolly-parton-net-worth.

37. Sara Blakely interview by Sarah AlBanna on a Stanford Graduate School of Business *View From The Top* podcast, April 2018, https://standord.io/2QDGBXU.

38. Strava, https://www.strava.com/get-started.

39. Thegeneralistlens, "Building a StoryBrand by Donald Miller (summary)," *Medium,* accessed October 27, 2023, https://thegeneralistlens.medium.com/building-a-storybrand-by-donald-miller-summary-99cc15ef650.

40. Easy IP, " Intellectual Property Protection for the New World," https://www.easyip.today/.

41. Kary Oberbrunner, "Welcome to the E-Mind™," podcast produced by Igniting Souls Media, https://ignitingsouls.com/emind/.

42. Jeff Goins, "Why You Should Practice Every Day for Two Years Before You Expect to Succeed," ©2022, accessed October 27, 2023, https://goinswriter.com/two-years/.

43. Jeff Goins, "A More Tasteful Alternative to Self-promotion: Practice in Public," *Copyblogger,* October 11, 2016, https://copyblogger.com/practice-in-public.

44. Attest, "12 Top Storytelling Marketing Examples: How Brands tell Stories," accessed July 28, 2023, https://www.askattest.com/blog/articles/12-top-storytelling-marketing-examples.

45. Kary Oberbrunner, Day Job to Dream Job (Powell, OH: Ethos Collective, 2018), 64.

46. "About Worms," https://www.worms4earth.com/a-snapshot-of-worm-biology?layout=left, accessed October 29, 2023.

47. Val d'Isère, "Iseran Pass," accessed on October 27, 2023, https://www.valdisere.com/en/val-disere-in-summer/cycle-tourism-and-vae/iseran-pass-and-route-des-grandes-alpes/.

48. Dangerous Roads. "Col de l'Iseran is the King of the Alps," accessed October 27, 2023, https://www.dangerousroads.org/europe/france/59-col-de-liseran-france.html.

49. Restoration Advisors, "The Value of a Bottle of Water," February 22, 2022, https://www.restorationadvisers.com/blog/waterbottle.

50. Dan Sullivan, "Why Finding Your Purpose Is The Key To Reaching Your Life Goals," *Strategic Coach,* accessed October 27, 2023, https://resources.strategiccoach.com/the-multiplier-mindset-blog/why-finding-your-purpose-is-the-key-to-reaching-your-life-goals-3.

51. Emma Cole, "Col du Granon: The climb that cracked Tadej Pogačar," *Cyclist,* November 1, 2022, https://www.cyclist.co.uk/in-depth/classic-climbs-col-du-granon.

52. Simon MacMichael, "Tour de France fans treated for hypothermia on Mont Ventoux," *Road.cc,* July 14, 2016, https://road.cc/content/news/197327-tour-de-france-fans-treated-hypothermia-mont-ventoux.

53. Rob Liu, "Intuition and how to trust your gut," *Lifeclub,* October 25, 2019, https://lifeclub.org/idea/intuition-trust-your-gut.

54. James Mangold & T-Bone Burnett. (2005) WALK THE LINE .

55. "Failogue: Steve Jobs was fired from Apple." *The Imperfectionist, a*ccessed October 27, 2023, https://imperfectionistblog.com/2015/04/failogue-1-steve-jobs/.

56. Unmistakable Creative, "Flow Boosts Your Productivity by 500% in 90 Minutes," April 3, 2023, https://unmistakablecreative.com/flow-productivity/.

57. Herbert Benson, M.D. and William Proctor, *The Breakout Principle: How to Activate the Natural Trigger That Maximizes Creativity, Athletic Performance, Productivity and Personal Well-Being* (New York: Scribner, 2023).

Acknowledgments

I'm extremely grateful for our incredible team at Igniting Souls and Blockchain Life. Thank you for always "dotting the i" and Showing Up Filled Up. It may not be easy to stay Souls on Fire, but we all know by now, it's so worth it.

Sarah Grandstaff, Jamie Chambers, Tanisha Williams, Melissa Fultz, Ruthie Bult, Travis Leonard, Travis White, Jill Ellis, Lori Piotrowski, Sheila Davis, Tony Colson, Elizabeth Haller.

About the Authors

Kary Oberbrunner

Dr. Kary Oberbrunner is a *Wall Street Journal* and *USA Today* bestselling author of more than a dozen books. As CEO of Igniting Souls and Blockchain Life, he helps authors, entrepreneurs, and influencers publish, protect, and promote their Intellectual Property and turn it into eighteen streams of income. His companies are committed to Setting Free World-Changing Ideas. An award-winning novelist, TEDx speaker, screenwriter, and inventor, he's been featured in *Forbes, Entrepreneur, CBS, Fox News, Yahoo,* and many other major media outlets.

As a young man, he suffered from severe stuttering, depression, and self-injury. Today a transformed man, Kary ignites souls. He speaks internationally on a variety of topics including leadership, personal growth, human performance, blockchain technology, and entrepreneurship. As a futurist, he often consults on marketing, branding, Intellectual Property, and Web3.

He has several earned degrees, including a Bachelor of Arts, Masters in Divinity, and Doctorate in Transformational Leadership. He also serves as the Berry Chair of Entrepreneurship at Cedarville University, where he teaches on the topics of Entrepreneurship and Digital Marketing. Kary enjoys cycling, especially in the French Alps. He lives in Ohio with his wife Kelly and three children: Keegan, Isabel, and Addison.

Lynne Modranski

Lynne Modranski is an author and inspirational speaker who loves to empower Christian leaders and inspire spiritual growth. She enjoys helping others discover their true identity and reach their full potential in Christ. Raised in an entrepreneurial environment, Lynne has always thrived partnering with small businesses to help run their offices and help with their branding. Nevertheless, her number one entrepreneurial endeavor has been the launch of her publishing company to house her own books.

Over the last twenty years, she's written several Bible Studies, devotionals, children's curricula, plays, and advent readings. In 2022, Lynne delved into the world of fiction and released her first novel, *Adira: Journey to Freedom*, a retelling of the story of Nehemiah from the eyes of his fictional niece. Wife to Steve, a local church pastor, Lynne is mom to Monica, Sylvia, and Julia and "Hada" to Joshua, Corryn, Elizabeth, and Jaycee.

Although she is a Worship Leader and Small Groups Coordinator at Sycamore Tree Church, Lynne is first and foremost a follower of Jesus Christ. She has a passion to help others find a real relationship with the One who has given her true life as she shows them how they can become the very best they can be in Christ Jesus!

CONNECT WITH KARY

Follow him on your favorite social media platforms today.

KaryOberbrunner.com

Made in the USA
Coppell, TX
12 November 2024